Twists and Turns

Personal Story Publishing Project Series

Bearing Up , 2018
- making do, bearing up, and overcoming adversity

Exploring , 2019
- discoveries, challenges, and adventures

That Southern Thing , 2020
- living, loving, laughing, loathing, leaving the South

Luck and Opportunity , sping 2021
- between if and if only

Trouble , fall 2021
- causing, avoiding, getting in, and getting out

Curious Stuff , spring 2022
- mementos, treasures, white elephants, and junk

Other selected titles by Randell Jones

Scoundrels, Rogues, and Heroes of the Old North State, 2004 & 2007
   by Dr. H.G. Jones, edited by Randell Jones & Caitlin Jones

Before They Were Heroes at King's Mountain, 2011

A Guide to the Overmountain Victory National Historic Trail, 2011,
   second edition, 2016

From Time to Time in North Carolina, 2017

Available through Daniel Boone Footsteps
www.danielboonefootsteps.com
1959 N. Peace Haven Rd., #105
Winston-Salem, NC 27106

Twists and Turns

Randell Jones, editor

Daniel Boone Footsteps
Winston-Salem, North Carolina

Copyrights retained by each writer for own stories
Permissions granted to Daniel Boone Footsteps
for publishing in this anthology

Compilation Copyright 2022, Daniel Boone Footsteps
All Rights Reserved

Daniel Boone Footsteps
1959 N. Peace Haven Rd., #105
Winston-Salem, NC 27106

RandellJones.com
DanielBooneFootsteps.com
DBooneFootsteps@gmail.com

*My life is one long curve,
full of turning points.*
— Pierre Trudeau,
Prime Minister of Canada

Preface

This book is the seventh in a series of anthologies, collections of personal stories on a set theme, our Personal Story Publishing Project. Since beginning in 2018, our collections have included the themes:
Bearing Up, "making do, bearing up, and overcoming adversity,"
Exploring, "discoveries, challenges, and adventure."
That Southern Thing, "living, loving, laughing, loathing, leaving the South."
Luck and Opportunity, "between if and if only"
Trouble, "causing, avoiding, getting in, and getting out," and,
Curious Stuff, "mementos, treasures, white elephants, and junk."

The book you are holding is the result of our seventh Call for Personal Stories, this one on the theme: "Twists and Turns—inflection points in life by choice, happenstance, misfortune, failure, and grace." We thank the scores of writers who responded to the call by submitting such interesting, thoughtful, and well-crafted stories. They delivered the diversity and depth of perspective we were hoping for and the humor and insight which proved we chose the right theme. Each story is targeted between 750 and 800 words, so the writers were challenged in executing their craft, telling an interesting story succinctly. The writers and we have all found the Personal Story Publishing Project through its seven iterations so far to be an instructive and rewarding writing experience. For the readers, it is a delight.

We received submissions from many writers in North Carolina and South Carolina, notably, but also from writers reaching across the country from Florida to the West Coast. We wish we could have printed them all, but we are delighted to continue curating stories for each collection, this time 50 stories.

In June 2019, we launched a second outlet for sharing the work of these fine writers with a broader audience. Their work can now be heard in our twice weekly podcast, "6-minute Stories." Our podcast is available through Apple Podcasts (iTunes), Spotify, and Stitcher. You can listen directly to "6-minute Stories" and find all the stories archived at RandellJones.com/6minutestories. Episodes are announced on Facebook @6minutestories.

Twists and Turns, the Personal Story Publishing Project, and "6-minute Stories" podcast are undertaken by author and publisher Randell Jones, doing business as Daniel Boone Footsteps in Winston-Salem, North Carolina.

Thank you for enjoying and appreciating good storytelling. And, remember…
  Everybody loves a good story.[sm] •

Contents

Preface — vii
Contents — ix-xv
Introduction — xvii

Confessions of an Ex-Poetry Editor — 1
    by Ruth Moose, Albemarle, NC
    — *"Read the poem again and call me back."*

The Bus Children — 5
    by Becky Gould Gibson, Wilmington, NC
    — *She looked like an angel.*

Capers in the Convent and a Sinner's Surprise — 9
    by Mary Alice Dixon, Charlotte, NC
    — *What would Nancy Drew do?*

Fugitive Spirits — 13
    by Gail Tyson, Knoxville, TN
    — *I crossed the threshold, feeling summoned.*

No More Kisses
    by Annette Brown, Atwater, CA — 17
    — *we're too old*

The Misunderstood Adventures of Godfrey Saddler — 21
    by Eric D. Johnson, Hilton Head Island, SC
    — *"Get your dumb ass off that child."*

Medusa's Diary   25
     by Rose-Mary Harrington, Wilmington, NC
     — *There isn't an antidote for a Mamushi.*

Metamorphosis   29
     by Catherine C. Con, Greer, SC
     — *respect for her sprouted*

Poor James   33
     by Mary Clements Fisher, Cupertino, CA
     — *Pity made a sour substitute for love.*

Homeless in LA   37
     by Jill Amber Chafin, Chapel Hill, NC
     — *What now?*

They Don't Leave Us   41
     by Lorraine Martin Bennett, Hayesville, NC
     — *waiting for a breeze, a storm, a sudden gale*

Philadelphia to Wilson   45
     by Ginny Foard, Sullivan's Island, SC
     — *I can't miss the bus.*

At 5 and 95, Mother Was a Star   49
     by Arlene Mandell, Linville, NC
     — *Word spread, and everyone came to watch.*

The Tattoo   53
     by Brooke Dupree, Easley, SC
     — *the only one I could not cover up*

Grabbing for the American Dream — 57
    by Akira Odani, St. Augustine, FL
    — *Can I help you? I speak some English.*

The Power Drill — 61
    by Lynne E Williams, Charlotte, NC
    — *Zhirrrrrr! Shirrrrrr! Bzzrrrrrr!*

Our Wedding Plan — 65
    by Vicki Easterly, Lexington, KY
    — *till death do us part*

A Soldier's Choice — 69
    by Lubrina Burton, Lexington, KY
    — *no soldier left behind*

The Hounds of Antigua — 73
    by Wayne A. Barnes, San Diego, CA
    — *ferocious, vicious, feral dogs trained to attack*

Flooded — 77
    by Tara Thompson, Durham, NC
    — *I'm running out of time.*

All Things Considered — 81
    by Lois Elizabeth Hicks, Ramseur, NC
    — *Well, that wasn't so bad, he thought.*

The Space Between — 85
    by David Inserra, Hilton Head Island, SC
    — *doors will open, and I will be set free*

Contents

A Tap at My Door — 89
  by Rebecca S. Holder, Winston-Salem, NC
  – *Help me?*

Should I Go or Should I Stay — 93
  by Emily Rosen, Boca Raton, FL
  – *I decided to play "Russian Roulette."*

The Thing About Life — 97
  by Alexandra Goodwin, Coral Springs, FL
  – *Two armed police officers escorted me out.*

Dark Water — 101
  by Barbara Houston, Charlotte, NC
  – *She grabbed me, pulled me under.*

Morgan: Our Escape Artist — 105
  by Janet K. Baxter, Kings Mountain, NC
  – *Don't fence me in.*

Putting Everything on the Line — 109
  by Deirdre Garr Johns, Hilton Head Island, SC
  – *It was a "yes" I feared.*

The Saltwater Taffy Escapade — 113
  by Patricia E. Watts, Mountville, SC
  – *not much comfort*

Right Turn at a Funeral — 117
  by M.J. Norwood, East Bend, NC
  – *I knew, right then, what I had to do.*

Kitty Gets a Name — 121
    by Joel R. Stegall, Winston-Salem, NC
    – *Anything that poops in my car has my attention.*

A Divine Dating Detour — 125
    by Sarah H. Clarke, Charlotte, NC
    – *the intriguing stranger*

One Day's Notice — 129
    by Ken Chamlee, Mills River, NC
    – *We'll call you.*

Losing Sight — 133
    by Marci Spencer, Old Fort, NC
    – *Visibility appeared endless.*

Finding Home — 137
    by Karen Luke Jackson, Flat Rock, NC
    – *No place is forever.*

A Mountain and a Girl — 141
    by Jim Riggs, Hilton Head Island, SC
    – *I was in over my head.*

November Wind — 145
    by Bob Amason, St. Augustine, FL
    – *a school of hard knocks*

This Much I Understand — 149
    by Wendy A. Miller, Portland, OR
    – *We tried to communicate in toddler French.*

Signposts 153
    by Annie McLeod Jenkins, Winston-Salem, NC
    — *living hand-to-mouth, skiing every day*

Heart and Soul 157
    by Bill Donohue, Winston-Salem, NC
    — *typically, sweet and mischievous*

Christmas 1970 161
    by Rosemary James, Richmond, KY
    — *and never leave you again*

Love in the Clouds 165
    by Phyllis Castelli, Henderson, NC
    — *like trying to save a handful of magic*

The Befuddled Entrepreneur 169
    by Valerie Macon, Fuquay-Varina, NC
    — *"What else could go wrong today?"*

Telling Eyes 173
    by Suzanne Cottrell, Oxford, NC
    — *If only I had known this earlier.*

New Trajectory 177
    by R.V. Kuser, Winston-Salem, NC
    — *My disability was always mentioned first.*

Make It Through 181
    by Leigh Anne Whittle, Snow Camp, NC
    — *My family is fine.*

At the Ocean's Edge   185
    by Paula Teem Levi, Clover, SC
    – *It was, indeed, my lucky day.*

Wild Mouse   189
    by Howard Pearre, Winston-Salem, NC
    – *Keep your eyes on the road, Sir.*

Curiosity Led to Dad's Calling   193
    by Monica Lee, Jonestown, TX
    – *He always wanted to know why!*

Nothing an Hour of Surfing Can't Fix   197
    by Randell Jones, Winston-Salem, NC
    – *"I hope it's not Bry Dog."*

Introduction

"It was a dark and stormy night. Suddenly, a shot rang out! A door slammed. The maid screamed. Suddenly, a pirate ship appeared on the horizon!"

I remember that tortured opening, or something similar, from a *Peanuts* cartoon by Charles Shultz as the intrepid beagle Snoopy labored atop his doghouse banging out on his typewriter the next great American novel. Snoopy has, perhaps, inspired more than a few would-be writers.

"Suddenly" is a word writers cautiously consider using, it too often serving as a trite means to redirect the reader to another line of thinking, to change the scene, the mood, the purpose, the outcome. Yet that word describes too accurately at times the lives we live, doesn't it? Suddenly, the rain began, the car came out of nowhere, the wolf lunged, my heart sank, love struck. Suddenly, it was over.

Our lives are peppered with sudden events—twists and turns that intercede and interrupt our supposedly intentional living. They are the inflection points in life that create an intervention leaving us and others changed on the other side.

Our lives plod on or speed by, depending upon our moods and what we are looking forward to or trying to avoid. Life can be, as they say in *The History Boys*, "just one damn thing after another." And so it goes until we stop and take a breath. We stand off to the side of whatever path we are on and look back up the trail of our lives so far. We might not have seen that jog in our path while we were on it so earnestly moving forward, but now that bend seems like the point in the journey where clearly everything changed—a twist, as it were. Or that jog in the path was actually a treefall that barely missed us, a rockslide we somehow escaped, or a sink hole that swallowed us up, the interruption in our journey unmistakable and unforgettable—a remarkable turn of events indeed. For better, for worse, for a moment, forever, our lives are products of twists and turns.

We are gratified by the response to our 7th Call for Personal Stories, and we are grateful to all the writers who invested time and energy into crafting personal stories for possible inclusion in this anthology. From among the submissions, we chose stories to include based on the quality of the writing and the resonance of the personal experiences shared with the announced theme, "Twists and Turns—inflection points in life by choice, happenstance, misfortune, failure, and grace."

In this collection, we have stories of challenge: climbing from despair a half-world away to succeed at the American Dream; reliving the *Grapes of Wrath*-life in real time every day. We have stories of compassion: opening your heart when you open your door to someone standing there in need; coming to grips for a lifetime with the consequences of one foolish decision.

Other stories explore our humanity and our connections: bursting with childish good intentions, innocent girls confront a reality their privileged lives had not imagined; a young man touches the hearts of those all around him from on-stage and behind the scenes.

Stories of gratitude and love abound: surprised to survive a medical mishap for no reason she can imagine but grace and luck; showing a little skin—especially this tattoo—changes her evening, and her life; waiting for the wind to blow and the violets to bloom so she can visit with family; a toddler's declaration of independence falters in the face of mother's hugs and kisses; and, a shot-gun wedding affirms the age-old promise of bride and groom.

And, of course, we enjoy light-hearted and heart-felt stories, too: imagining what Nancy Drew would do if she too were a sinner; a fear of limbless reptiles snakes its way across generations; one clever canine, who knows exactly who he is in the world, continually escapes the repeated and pitiful attempts to fence him in; and one gentle soul brings animal rescue to the streets, rain or shine.

These are some of the stories among those we share in this collection, looking back, staring up the road we have traveled thus far and remembering how we got here, where we went alone and when together with others. And "why"—the big question. Why did we do that, go one way and not the other, choose this path and not that one? Was it always our choice to make or did circumstances, fate, providence, or others make those choices for us? And afterward, what did we choose to do, or not, about it?

Choices. That's what we made at each twist and at each turn. And lessons are what we learned along the way, lessons to remind ourselves for the next time, lessons to pass along to those who find themselves on their own paths, trying to decide which way they might go and why—for better or worse, for now or forever.

And then suddenly, here we are, banging out a story about another dark and stormy night. But that's what we choose to do. It's who we have learned to be. Because we are writers.

Speaking for myself, Thanks, Snoopy. •

RJ

Confessions of an Ex-Poetry Editor
by Ruth Moose

You don't sign on with a new little magazine, maybe ANY little magazine, expecting to be paid. Little magazines struggle from Day One, go under in weeks and months. Figure it's experience under your belt and/or maybe giving back to your profession. Plus, it will add some credibility to your Curriculum Vitae. Not a bad thing. And besides, you have a hole in your life this adventure might help fill.

After a long marriage, my husband had just died. A five-year illness filled with hospitals, doctor's visits, treatments, all. Depression followed and dealing with mountain-size grief. Teaching three days a week, student papers kept me sane, but weekends were another story. I had time to fill. So, I signed on with *The Village Rambler*, a two-person masthead; Dave as publisher, photographer, and interviewer; Elizabeth, editor. Ink on both their MFA degrees from Boston College still wet. They were young and fun, and *The Village Rambler* was a dream on their kitchen table two blocks away from me. I could walk over once a week or Dave would bring me a handful of poems and I'd pick one or two. I'd take the rest back for Elizabeth to tuck in a rejection note and return.

The Rambler had no ads and I referred to it as "the daughter of *The Sun*" a long-established, left-wing sort of, publication of Sy Sfransky in Chapel Hill that had national recognition. Dave's first interview and photographs were of a renown potter in Chatham County. Nicely done. And Elizabeth tucked in a poem I'd chosen, presented it beautifully full page, plus filled in a shorter poem at the end of an article on the local, and just established, arts council. Around town *The Rambler* was sold from a stand in the village soda shop and a local eatery. I didn't know how many copies were sold or how many subscribers there were. All I did was read the poems submitted and what surprised me was how many good poets there were out there, poets I had never read nor heard of. And I liked to think I read widely and well.

By now *The Rambler* offices had moved to the upper floor of a historic hotel downtown Pittsboro and every Friday afternoon I'd pop in, pick up the week's submissions for my Sunday night reading.

Every Sunday night I'd get in pajamas, pillows against headboard, poems surrounded me. Submissions had picked up mightily since Elizabeth listed *The Rambler* with some writers' sites as well as *Writers' Digest Market Guide* and *Yearbook*. Now I got at least two large, brown paper grocery bags stacked full of poems. Poems! From every corner of the universe, mostly places I'd never heard of, countries I didn't know existed.

The Rambler, now picking up status, had an intern who opened envelopes, removed cover letters, paper clipped them BEHIND the submitted poems, and stacked them for my pickup. This hands-on work let me leap right into the poems, and if I saw something I liked, I read the cover letters. Most publications I'd never heard of, but was delighted to know that in Podunk, Illinois, there was such and such a publication, that maybe a lot of arts councils were funding literary magazines. This was cheering because at one point, through a local arts council, I had edited a little magazine, *The Uwharrie Review*, and I'm sure 99% of the world never heard of it, but I published some good poetry and gave a lot of fledgling poets a place to get work into print and maybe into the hands of readers/other poets.

I had a couple of "challenges" with Elizabeth when I'd run into a friend whose poem I had accepted for *The Rambler* only to have it "returned" a few days later with a nice letter saying it would not be published. No explanation. Well, I certainly wanted one and quickly got in touch with Elizabeth who said she, as editor, had the right to overrule my choices. I was stung. We had obvious differences in poetry taste, but I did ask her to let me know before she overruled me. I certainly didn't like being put in the middle and having to apologize when I ran into someone who had submitted to *The Rambler*.

The next challenge came when Elizabeth called to tell me they would not run a poem I had just accepted called "The Gospel According to Elvis."

"Why ever not?"

She explained *The Rambler*'s policy not to run religious material. I nearly dropped the phone laughing.

"Read the poem again and call me back."

Confessions of an Ex-Poetry Editor

The poem was a spoof. Very funny and full of puns and plays on words. I loved it. She called me back, but not laughing. Said she would run the Elvis poem, but it would be against her better judgement. I had to insist she run the Elvis poem. A few months later after the issue had been out a week or so and gotten around a bit, she called me again.

"Can you find us another poem like the Elvis one?"

I laughed, said I'd love to, but it didn't work that way. The Elvis poet even submitted again and none of these poems were accepted. They just didn't seem to hit the mark the way the Elvis one had.

One night several years into my "job" as poetry editor, I read a poem that made me think of something else I'd read by this poet. I flipped back to the cover letter. He wrote, "Thank you for the $25 check for my poem *so-and-so-and-so* which you ran in a *whatever* issue." I read it again. Again. *What?* The Rambler *was paying poets? But* NOT *the poetry editor!* Well, we'd see about that.

Monday morning, arming myself with restrained animosity, I stood at Elizabeth's desk and quietly presented my case. Of course writers should be paid. But shouldn't Poetry Editors be paid as well? It was honorable work, but work, nevertheless. She said she and Dave had never paid themselves a salary, but since I asked, they would take my position into consideration. A few days later, she called to say I would be paid, but it wouldn't be much, and it would not be retroactive.

It wasn't and what I began to be paid was true, as she said, not much, but I did continue as Poetry Editor until the magazine was discontinued. Dave and Elizabeth moved to another area, had a baby then another and I've lost touch. I don't think *The Village Rambler* ever made any money. There were never any ads, and subscribers must have been scant. Most little magazines are a labor of love. And I did love reading some really good poetry and wished *The Rambler* could have published more. And paid more: poets and poetry editor alike. •

Copyright 2022, Ruth Moose

Ruth Moose was on the Creative Writing faculty at the University of North Carolina-Chapel Hill for 15 years. She has published three collections of short stories, *The Wreath Ribbon Quilt*, *Dreaming in Color*, and *Neighbors and Other Strangers* with individual stories in numerous publications including in Holland, South Africa, England, and Denmark. Moose has published six collections of poetry, most recently, *The Librarian and Other Poems* and *Tea*. She received a MacDowell Fellowship, a North Carolina Artist Fellowship and a prestigious Chapman Award for Teaching.

Her most recent novel *The Goings on at Glen Arbor Acres* is from St. Andrews University Press, a small press 50 years old in Laurinburg, North Carolina. Her novel, *Doing It at the Dixie Dew*, her first novel, won the Malice Domestic prize for a first traditional mystery and was published by St. Martin's Press in 2014, with a sequel, *Wedding Bell Blues*, in 2016. Ruth lives in Albemarle, North Carolina, where she grew up and where her sons and families live.

TWISTS AND TURNS

The Bus Children
by Becky Gould Gibson

Claudia and I always sat in the middle row the first year we rode the bus from the county to the "consolidated" school in town. We were in fourth grade. I was still wondering what *consolidated* meant. We jabbered nonstop (*What did The Little Moron say when … ?*) until we got to the billboard for Sunbeam Bread. There was Little Miss Sunbeam, grinning big as life in her blue dress with a white ruffled collar and her blonde curls tied up with a blue ribbon. She could have been one of us.

The bus took a right and clattered down a dirt road to a ramshackle house, not a speck of paint on it. We all got quiet. A brother and sister crossed the bare yard to the bus, grabbed the metal handrail and pulled themselves up. A boy on the aisle said *pee-yew*, holding his nose. Her dress and his pants must've come from the donation box at some church. They didn't smile or speak to any of us.

Nobody on the bus was rich. But it didn't take a genius to figure out who was better off. Claudia and I got the bright idea of taking up a collection. It was a cold clear day right before Christmas. We sat in our usual spot. No way Santa

Claus would ever come to *that* house. (I knew who Santa was. Claudia had let the cat out of the bag in third grade.) We planned a trip to Ben Franklin, the dime-store on the square.

We were pretty pleased with ourselves. Just from kids on the bus and with what Claudia and I put in, we got a whole big bag of pennies, nickels, dimes, even a few quarters. The store had high ceilings and bins made of wood and dark old floors that smelled like cleaning oil. We weighed our choices and counted our money. For the boy, a plastic car or truck? (The wooden train cost too much.) For the girl, our hearts were set on a Dy-Dee doll that drinks and wets and comes in a box with a see-through window. I'd do the wrapping myself.

Finally, the Friday afternoon before Christmas vacation. I'd brought the paper sack of presents that morning and hid it all day under my desk. On the way out of the school parking lot, Claudia and I could barely contain ourselves. We came to the familiar turn. The bus driver was in on it. He'd wait while we trailed the kids to the house. By the time we got to the porch, even before we went in, I felt a knot in my throat.

I'd seen plenty of tarpaper shacks on the way to Pawleys. But I'd never ever been inside one. My parents talked a lot about not having any money, what with the drought and the farm not paying off. But if we were poor, our poor was nothing like this.

The mother came out. A scrawny woman in a faded shift, thin sweater pulled over her belly and a child on one hip. Before we knew it, we were through the front door and in a room with a small window, a fireplace angled across one corner and lath walls covered in yellowed newspaper. The place reeked of fatback and collards.

I couldn't take my eyes off the mantel. On it was a framed photograph of a child-sized casket—pure white and lined in white satin. Inside, a little girl dressed in white was propped up on a white satin pillow. She looked like an angel. Everything up there was white, even the plastic roses covered in dust. I thought of the altar in church.

No one I knew would take a picture of a dead baby. Much less put it out where everybody could see it. It didn't take me long to realize we were out of our depth. I remember pride in the eyes of that woman as she stood facing us with her children. She took the sack and mumbled *thank you*. We couldn't get out of there fast enough. We ran, our faint *merry christmas* floating behind us. We climbed in and the bus doors wheezed shut.

How little I knew of what people wanted. The mother's stiff *thanks*, the children's bewildered silence. I still think of entering that house with our cheap toys and tacky kindness, only to remind them of what they could not buy for themselves. We'd brought our innocent offerings from the blonde world of the Sunbeam girl, as if a darker world did not exist. We'd meant to make the children happy. We were met with blank looks.

We had trespassed. •

The Bus Children

Copyright 2022, Becky Gould Gibson

Becky Gould Gibson has published eight collections of poetry, notably, *Aphrodite's Daughter* (Texas Review Press, 2007); *Need-Fire* (Bright Hill Press, 2007); *Heading Home* (Main Street Rag, 2014); *The Xanthippe Fragments* (Saint Andrews Review Press, 2016); and *Indelible* (The Broadkill River Press, 2018). Her current focus is creative nonfiction. Two short pieces have appeared in print, one in *Canary*, another in *Snowy Egret*. Becky Gibson taught English at Guilford College until her retirement in 2008. She lives in Wilmington, North Carolina.

Capers in the Convent and a Sinner's Surprise
by Mary Alice Dixon

"When I grow up, I'm gonna be a Sister of Mercy nun and a Nancy Drew detective," I declared to my mom in 1963.

"I don't want to discourage you, but you know what they say, the best laid plans," she paraphrased her favorite Robert Burns poem, "often go astray." Mom sighed, knowing I was smitten with both elaborate costumes and mysteries featuring girl detectives. "Life has a way of surprising us, Honey."

But I knew exactly how my life would turn out. After all, I was 12.

In their long black tunics and starched white wimples, the Sisters of Mercy who ran my small North Carolina school looked like magicians. And they were as fearless as Nancy Drew, especially Sister Jean, the principal. She once climbed a fire escape, crawled through a classroom window, yelled "Surprise," then handed out a pop quiz. I adored that woman.

"Sister Jean," I announced, "I want to be a nun. And a detective."

She stared at me through wire-rimmed glasses. "Get back to me in ten years."

I remained undiscouraged. After all, Nancy Drew would never give up. She'd climb hidden staircases, explore locked attics, solve any problem. Nothing stopped her. Nothing would stop me. Like I said, I was 12.

My opportunity to sample both professions soon came.

"You have an assignment," Sister Jean said. "I'd like you to water the convent poinsettias during Christmas break. All the sisters will be gone."

"Yes, Sister."

"The poinsettias are in our chapel, ground floor."
"Yes, Sister."

"Upstairs is cloistered. It's a sin if you go up there. Understood?"
"Yes, Sister."
She handed me the "keys to the kingdom."

A day later I walked across the dirt field separating my family's backyard from the convent. Unlocking the door, I entered the chapel. Beside the altar stood a tall lit sanctuary candle, its sacred blaze signaling God's presence. Sister Jean didn't tell me the nuns would dare leave a candle burning with nobody home. They sure were women of faith.

"Sorry, God," I said, blowing out his holy flame, feeling like Judas.

A dozen pale poinsettias stood near the altar. I watered each slowly, testing the potting soil, making sure the roots didn't drown. Like any good detective, I was curious about the forbidden rooms. But I stayed in the chapel.

Second day, same pattern. Until I heard scratching from above.

I knew it wasn't God talking to me, though he was probably pretty mad about his candle. Maybe squirrels?

What would Nancy do? I asked myself. A nun would obey orders, but a detective would investigate. A nun who was also a detective? She'd save her convent from squirrels. I bet Sister Jean would, too.

The scratching stopped as I crept upstairs. I looked in the sisters' spartan bedrooms, their vows of poverty in evidence, though not the source of the scratching. Do squirrels hide in mattresses? I bounced on a bed. Only the wood squeaked, only a slight crack appeared in the frame.

"Sorry, God," I said, already on the devil's slippery slope.

I developed a routine. Each day I'd tend the poinsettias, sometimes pinching them back so they wouldn't grow leggy. Then, mystery sounds or not, I'd explore upstairs, drawn especially to the sisters' medieval garments. The first starched wimple I tried on itched something awful. Second one, too. Wool robes felt leaden. Black veils, heavy. For a sinner, I had a lot of complaints.

Still, I tended the poinsettias carefully, rotating the clay pots to insure each got the right amount of morning sun, watching their pink fronds deepen to red.

One day after playing dress-up more than detective, I left a veil and a wimple crumpled on a bed. "Sorry, God. I'll tidy up tomorrow."

That night the nuns returned.

Monday morning Sister Jean called me to her office. I was scared.

Capers in the Convent and a Sinner's Surprise

"Did you go upstairs?"
I was a sinner but not a liar. "Yes, Sister."

"And?"
"Maybe I heard squirrels?"

"Find any?"
"No, Sister."

"What do you have to say for yourself, young lady?"
"How're your poinsettias?"

"Best they've ever looked." She smiled. "And God bless you for blowing out that candle."

A week later I spotted gray squirrels on the convent roof. "Now you show up," I muttered.

I discovered my mother was right about plans. I was wrong. I wasn't cut out to be a nun, though I still cherish the memory of Sister Jean. I wasn't cut out to be a detective, though I still love mystery stories. But, to my surprise, I also discovered I'm not so bad with houseplants and I'm definitely the sinner you want around when there's an unattended candle left burning in your house.•

Copyright 2022, Mary Alice Dixon

Mary Alice Dixon lives in Charlotte, NC, where she is a hospice volunteer, former professor, and happy member of Charlotte Writers Club and Charlotte Lit. She is a Pushcart nominee, *Pinesong Award* winner, *Broad River Review Rash Award in Poetry* finalist, and *LIT/south* fiction finalist. Her work appears in four PSPP anthologies and is in or forthcoming from *Amethyst Review, Chicken Soup for the Soul, Kakalak, Main Street Rag, moonShine review, Mythic Circle* and elsewhere. Mary Alice collects hats, mysteries, and houseplants.

Fugitive Spirits
by Gail Tyson

On a visit to my ancestral homeland, Ireland, I had no intention of visiting Europe's youngest cathedral. I've long preferred medieval architecture. But a ramble around Galway brought me to the Cathedral of Our Lady Assumed into Heaven and St. Nicholas. Colossal limestone, completed in 1965, it shouldered a dome that glowed ruddy gold on a morning the Irish call fierce (very) mild. *Why not go inside?*

Massive double doors at the west entrance bore nine bronze relief plaques, which told the stories of the Gospels, the miracles, and the martyrs of the early Christian faith. They measured the size of one to three handspans, crafted so tenderly that I longed to touch them—refraining out of respect for works of art. Here waves whorled around a boat, its sail tilted over three terrified disciples; Jesus, straighter than the mast, outstretched his palm, cupping the dense energy of scrolling water. Nearby a fish dove, its tail patterned like a labyrinth, fins spiraled. Beside it, Jesus healed the paralyzed man lowered from a rooftop: the stranger's kinsman grimaced, straining; the paralytic's face so vulnerable; Jesus' head bent as if from the weight of his halo. I crossed the threshold, feeling summoned.

Inside I learned the cathedral sits on the former site of the City Jail. This spiritual sanctuary was deliberately raised, as a former bishop of Galway wrote, in a "place of darkness, pain, and human suffering." Beneath my feet: sepia marble quarried in Connemara. Over my head: a coffered timber ceiling of red cedar. Above the altar: a dome resting on four pillars adorned with mosaic torsos of archangels. Their glittering, widespread wings lifted my eyes even higher to a vault of indigo.

Vast as Limbo, hushed as a sepulcher, smelling faintly of tallow—this hallowed space slowed my stride. The souls of those who perished here seeped from the shadows: the men who fought for Ireland's independence, the debtors, the petty thieves. After execution, jailkeepers buried the bodies in quicklime. A large white cross marked the site where their bones dissolved.

Turnkeys disposed of those prisoners—once impassioned, overwhelmed, desperate human beings—completely, efficiently. Their unlived lives lingered, filling my throat as if each one sought a voice. Hair on my arms stood up, skin conducting to my marrow the emotional currents of fear, anger, despair that still dwelled here.

Shaken by so much longing, I drew close to a sculpture of the Virgin. Expecting the placid composure and Western attributes distilled over centuries of Mary-making, her face stunned me.

It melded Asian, African, and Caucasian features, like a multiracial Millennial with an enigmatic expression. What kind of artist could imagine this icon in such a fresh, compelling way? It turned out a German immigrant, Imogen Stuart, had sculpted this figure and cast the bronze plaques on the west doors. Arriving in Ireland in 1948, the 22-year-old found her creative homeland, later telling a journalist, "I knew this was my country. I was totally taken over by Irish art: the landscape, the ruins, the history of the saints and scholars."

I felt a kinship with her. Visit after visit, Ireland has allayed my experience of displacement, brought on by my moves from one city to another. This island returns me to "the place where you come back to yourself," in the words of Irish poet John O'Donohue.

As I stood in that lapis light, I felt confused. How could I sense homecoming on a site raised as a "parable of absolution"? For me, a cradle Catholic, forgiveness has always collided with what I thought I deserved. Time and again, though, unexpected mercies have brought what was lost back to life. A memory hovered: *suffering* derives from the etymological root *bher*—to bear/endure, also to bear children, as if suffering can produce new life.

"Have you clung to your grief because it is all you have left?" I asked the fugitive spirits. I told them how, for a long time, grief held me fast to the love and a life that vanished in weeks. How, in the wake of that death, the holding seared me like bullets taken in the name of freedom. Felt as hard as a few

Fugitive Spirits

coins owed. Smelled fresh as a shirt snatched off a line of washing. "Let it go," I murmured to the souls who died here. "You are not forgotten."

Did my prayer cauterize their wounds, unravel the tethers of grief? All I know is this: The dust motes spinning around me, the light glinting on mosaic angels, felt like spirits rising and shining. I carried their stories down the aisle and bore them, light as air, across the threshold, leaving the place, a short time ago, I had no desire to visit. •

Copyright 2022, Gail Tyson

The luck of the Irish brought Gail Tyson to Knoxville, Tennessee, in fall 2021, where she belongs to the Knoxville Writers Guild and the Pre-Pulitzer Critique Group. In 2020 Shanti Arts published her chapbook, *The Vermeer Tales*. Current and upcoming work appears in *Rockvale Review*, *Still: the Journal*, *Psaltery & Lyre*, and *Thimble Literary Magazine*. Gail serves as president of the board of Knoxville's Flying Anvil Theatre, where she paints sets and avoids giving curtain talks.

No More Kisses
by Annette Brown

I hover over my son Cole, who is wiggling into the car seat, when he makes a life-changing declaration: "Mom," he sighs. "Mom, I'm too old for kisses. So, no more kisses... I mean it. No. More." He points his finger on "no" and "more" as I jerk my eyes from the car-seat strap to his face.

"What?"

"Justin never lets his mom kiss him."

"So?" I ask, clicking the buckle in place.

"He told me we're too old." He exhales. "So, no more kisses." He swings his feet in rhythm with his words.

No more kisses. My eyes widen and brows furrow. *What does he mean he's too old? He's 4! When did 4 become old? Who is this Justin kid anyway?*

I look in the rearview mirror. The sun shining through the back window is blinding, adding to my jostling emotions. *What about our goodnights? Our goodbyes? Our hellos?* A sudden hollowing brushes my stomach. I feel like I am losing something precious, something I have known all along might be temporary. I know independence is the goal, but it's too soon.

"Wow. No more kisses. That's big." I pull from the curb thinking about his creamy cheeks, so soft they scream for kisses. Cole is quirky. He will only wear certain clothes—and shorts forever unless I put my foot down. *It's winter. Pants only!* He loves to be independent. Now he has terms. Terms taste sour in my mouth. I want to shake my head no. I am not ready for terms.

Ready or not, I am faced with Cole's declaration. Should I honor it? I kiss my parents in greeting and goodbye. We hug. We touch. It's how we show love. Should I demand smooches from Cole, make it a fight, or save struggle for non-negotiables, crucial issues of safety or wellbeing?

At the stop light, I relax my grip on the steering wheel and focus on Cole in the mirror: summer-sky clear eyes, unsettled waves of blonde curls. A stress ache grips my shoulders. *Breathe*, I remind myself. I am slow to respond.

"I still kiss grandma and grandpa."
Cole says nothing.
"I still kiss your brother Matt and he's 8."
Cole says nothing, determination scrunching his face.
"Okay, no more kisses."

"Good!" he exclaims with a single head nod, punctuating his conviction.

The light turns green. I imagine sneak kiss-attacks when Cole's settled in the bathtub or snug in the car seat, but I know I am unlikely to launch such an attack. I have agreed to his request.

Our morning routine changes: "Just a hug, Mom," he reminds me after I kiss Matt goodbye. Our bedtime routine changes: "No, kisses," Cole warns, waving a hand back and forth as I kneel to tuck in his blankets.

Days become weeks, and our routine becomes no-kisses. Attending to our busy schedules fills my mind, and I think little about the change. So today my eyebrows lift a little as Cole crawls into my lap and interrupts my reading.

"What ya doin'?"

"I was reading. What are you doing?"

"Nothin.'"

"Just decided to come in?"

"Yeah."

We sit quietly for a moment until Cole turns to face me, a smirk spreading slowly across his face, eyes a-twinkle. He stares a moment. "Mom, I told you...no more kisses." Then he abruptly turns to look straight ahead, giving me his cheek.

"I kn...." I stop. I am not kissing him. Nor am I thinking about kissing him. But his cheek tempts. "What?" I ask innocently, an equally devilish grin tickling my face.

"I told you," his eyes edging sideways, "no more kisses." With that, he turns his entire face and stares at me wide-eyed, burying his smile beneath pin-point freckles. Then he leans in

No More Kisses

slowly. I lean in until our foreheads touch. We erupt in laughter, and I sink my nose into his cheek, launching a smooch attack.

A wave of giggles washes over us, warms us, lifts us. Finally, I stop and our giggles trail from the room. We sit panting from the laughter and silliness. Until he turns to me again, the same twinkle tinting his eyes, "Mom, I told you, No…More…Kisses!"

We fritter away half an hour playing this game. Each of us delighted by our part.

Cole took a step toward independence, making a small change that felt monumental in the context of our family. I responded with acceptance—buried my sense of loss. Cole responded with a test to determine whether he's allowed to step back. Of course, he is. I'll be there. That's what we do as parents—kisses or no kisses. Above all, we hold on white-knuckle tight because parenthood is a ride fraught with stomach-clenching drops, hair-whipping wind, and cheek-stretching smiles—the best kind. •

Copyright 2022, Annette Brown

Annette L. Brown lives in Atwater, California on an almond farm where she has been writing for her own pleasure for over 30 years. Following her recent retirement from teaching, she has become serious about refining her craft and to this end feels privileged to be part of two writing groups: the Taste Life Twice Writers and the Light Makers' Society. Annette is inspired by nature, family, beauty, and humor. Pieces reflecting those inspirations have been published in *Cathexis Northwest Press* and a local newspaper.

The Misunderstood Adventures of Godfrey Saddler
by Eric D. Johnson

Godfrey was bred to instill fear—historically in wolves, but more recently in delivery people, cyclists, small animals, and adolescent boys, which at that time included me. We were neighbors, but the few encounters we had involved him bolting from his yard baring giant yellow canines, his eyes focused on my jugular. My role involved climbing onto cars, garage roofs, and tree limbs until he went away.

I don't recall seeing Godfrey walking on a leash, giving me a sniff, or letting me scratch the back of his neck. He never developed the collegiality of the other neighborhood dogs like Dolly the Dachshund who liked to lay her long body in the middle of the street, or Nicholas Simpson Price the black Lab who could bark to three if you tossed him cookies. Maybe Godfrey had a thirst for freedom, adventure, or friendship, but his language of growls and snarls made him seem angry and aggressive.

Occasionally, for reasons I never grasped, he would escape his yard and run directly to our house. My mother supplemented her income by providing lunch to kids who attended the local elementary school. My guess is he was attracted to the children playing on our front lawn, small smelly animals darting across his territory. He would bound onto our property with his head to the ground, scattering frantic children. During one such foray, a 5-year-old boy became paralyzed by terror. By the time the kid decided to run, the big German Shepherd had knocked him down and stood over the whimpering child's body in what looked like triumph.

I watched the drama from atop the roof of Mom's Chevy Nova. I thought Godfrey might bite the kid's head off, as he had done, allegedly, to an opossum whose headless body was found in the middle of the street. But nothing happened. The dog stood over the boy and stared into space. My mother walked onto the front lawn wielding a broom, hissing, "Get your dumb ass off that child."

Godfrey lowered his head, sniffed the kid's crotch, and trotted home.

My mom talked to Godfrey's mom, a statuesque woman named Cherry Saddler, about the incident. Godfrey stood obediently by Ms. Cherry's side, occasionally easing next to my mother, and gently rubbing his body against her leg. My mother, having a complicated relationship with animals, kneed the brute out of the way. He was persistent, rubbing against her, sniffing her feet, and interposing himself between the two women. I couldn't completely hear the conversation, but there was laughter and talk about wigs, and food prices at the A&P.

This conference about him had no effect on Godfrey because

he escaped again. This time he made it to the C. W. Henry school where he rampaged through the school yard causing children to abandon their back packs, coats, and musical instrument cases as he herded them into a corner of the playground. He snarled menacingly at every teacher foolish enough to try to read his tags. The custodians would not go near him.

The principal asked, "Whose dog is this?"

One of my mother's lunchtime clients, muttered, "Auntie Neet?"

The principal retreated to the office and asked her all-knowing secretary, "Who is Auntie Neet? Her dog is terrorizing the school yard!"

The secretary knew that Juanita Johnson was the "Auntie Neet" in question and placed the call.

"Mrs. Johnson, your dog has gotten loose in our school yard and is causing a great deal of mischief. Could you please come and retrieve it?

"I don't own a dog," replied my mother who was busy planning lunch while keeping an eye on one of the toddlers she watched during the day.

"Well, one of our students says it's your dog."
"What kind of dog is it?"
"I believe it's the kind the police use, a German Shepherd."

The Misunderstood Adventures of Godfrey Saddler

"I bet that's Cherry Saddler's dog. She works in Center City. Just tell him to go home."

"He's causing quite a stir and we'll be forced to call the police if this continues."

My mother ended the call with resignation, "Ahhh, dammit!"

She drove to the school and found Godfrey prancing around, keeping his flock of frightened children pinned in the corner of the yard. She pulled over and rang the bell she used to call us into the house for dinner.

Godfrey heard the bell, looked in my mother's direction, then ambled over to the Nova.

My mother blew smoke from the cigarette lodged in the corner of her mouth, laughed, and said, "Wait till I tell Cherry. Get in, Fool."

Godfrey climbed into the back seat of the Nova and sat next to the toddler. Both dozed off during the short ride home. •

Copyright 2022, Eric D. Johnson

Eric D Johnson lives in Bluffton, South Carolina, where he is a member of the Island Writers Network. Eric is the author of *Run to Win* and has recently completed his second novel *A Second Coming*, due to launch in 2022. Eric has contributed to the anthology *Journey into My Brother's Soul* and two Island Writers Network anthologies, *Reflections* and *Ripples*. Eric enjoys life in the Lowcountry with his wife Gwen and fawning over his granddaughter Gia.

Medusa's Diary
by Rose-Mary Harrington

1958. My mother relates that in her early childhood years she lived in India during the Empire. My then 7-year-old mother was placed in the custody of a slender, tall Ayah, with a red dot on her forehead. Her Ayah taught her how to wrap a turban and how to curse in Hindi. She took my mother to Digha beach, where they would wade in tide pools, scouring for sea creatures. My mother casually overturned a large flat rock from which a 2-foot snake slid over her feet. My mother screamed. Her Ayah rushed to her with her sari flapping in the wind. When my mother would not stop screaming, her Ayah slapped her across her tear-stained face.

1963. My mother retells the snake story, but now the snake is three feet long.

1970. My mother repeats the snake episode during a visit with my future in-laws in America. The snake is now six feet long.

1972. My new husband has graduated from Navy flight school, and we are stationed in California. The squadron commander hosts a cocktail party. Upon arrival Captain Drexler asks my

husband to assist him with something in the garage. They disappear only to re-appear cradling a giant boa constrictor. The Captain wants everyone to stretch out his pet snake so he can take a Polaroid picture. I sneak into the hallway.
In the next room they are spreading the snake. I pop into the background just as Captain Drexler requests participants to smile, shouting, "Cheese, everyone."

Before this assignment, Captain Drexler had been the Russian interpreter for the President. He would have been on the hotline between the White House and the Kremlin. I wonder if the CIA knows he keeps a lethal weapon in his garage?

1977. We are deployed to Tokyo, Japan. We live on base. My 5-year-old son, Keir, is over at the Sanders house next door playing with their children. I hear an ambulance siren pulling up outside the Sanders'. I see Becky Sanders carrying Keir. "What's happened?" I yell.

Becky replies, "Keir and Scott were playing soccer in the back yard. Keir slipped and there was a Mamushi snake."
The doctor in the E.R. is known widely for his misdiagnoses. He stands calmly, peering over his Navy-issue spectacles staring at his wristwatch.

"How long ago did this happen?" he enquires.

"About five or six minutes." I "guesstimate."

He looks at me and announces, "There isn't an antidote for a Mamushi." The doctor continues matter-of-factly, "If it had been a Mamushi he would be dead by now."

2020. New house in North Carolina, a new husband. I venture into our shrub-enclosed secret garden with its 3-tiered fountain. I am enjoying this hidden place, with light and sun filtering through the trees to my back. I am reading an article on epigenetics, in which twins who were separated at birth share identical life choices. I am engrossed in the theory that genetic memory could be in our DNA and cellular structure. I notice a glint above the page. I peer up. Coiling itself around the fountain is a 7-foot golden snake. I inch my way to the opening and skedaddle into the house.

2021. I am in my home office one evening. My daughter, Ashley, is getting ready for the night shift at a fast-food establishment. I see my husband returning from work through my window. He enters by the front door. This is unusual; he always uses the back door. I join him in the den at 6:30 to watch the news. Ashley has gone off to sling hamburgers. My cell phone rings. Ashley's calling. She sounds ticked off.

"Tell Dad to sanitize the back door handle and to leave the front porch lights on. I am coming in the front door tonight."

"What are you talking about?" I ask.
There is a long pause.

"Dad didn't tell you?"
There is another pause.

"About the snake?" Ashley continues. "The snake that was wrapped around the back door handle?"

I am curt when I reply, "No, he did not."
I hang up the phone. My husband explains.

Medusa's Diary

"I knew you would be upset," he declares. "Besides, the snake wasn't that big."

I am riled. "Where is it now?" I enquire.

"I don't understand your phobia about snakes," he responds, somewhat bewildered.

He puts his arms around me. "You are a strong woman. You will figure this out."

At that moment I recall epigenetics and the passing of fears through molecular structure. Could my mother's childhood trauma be the culprit? In my dreams, my mother's snake is now 18 feet long.

Have I the right to blame my mother?
As all dutiful daughters do. •

Copyright 2022, Rose-Mary Harrington

Rose-Mary resides in Wilmington, North Carolina. Rose-Mary is a member of the Cape Fear Poetry and Prose Society and the Port City Playwrights Project. Her background is in theatre.
Rose-Mary's plays have been performed all over the Unites States and Great Britain. In 2018 her full-length play *Detained* was produced by Up Theatre, New York. Rose-Mary was winner of the New Playwrights Project by Utah Shakespeare Company for her play *Six Seconds*. Rose-Mary is a life member of the Dramatists' Guild. This is her first foray into short story writing.

Metamorphosis
by Catherine C. Con

A tall, clumsy woman, Mother slouched forward doing her bookkeeping business. She was quiet then, but not when she negotiated while doing her real estate investments.

"We can't keep up with her, can we?" I asked while my father and I prepared dinner together, listening to Mother on the phone arguing about the material for her flooring project. After dinner, I did homework with my father. Mother, in her office, concentrated on the books from her customers. She had two file organizers, one for the bookkeeping business, and one for real estate. During the economic boom in Seventies Taiwan, she got caught up with the climb.

I swore I would never have anything to do with real estate. At 15, I thought reading and writing were superior to money-making businesses. But at 34, with an 8-month-old infant, I started a small business of real estate investment in The Crescent City with my mother.

It was a humble beginning in New Orleans—a broken door one-bedroom condo with peeled paint.

"To practice," my mother said.

Wood flooring samples and paint color cards crammed together in the diaper bag with baby toys, formula bottles, burping cloth, all accompanied me during this initiation ritual into American entrepreneurship. Even with Mother's support, it was a frantic time. A small business can demand all your time and energy. So will a baby.

"Buildings and people. That would decide the success or failure of the business," Mother told me after I had problems with a tenant.

"Different cultures. You need to learn to manage people and that is the hardest part of any business," my mother instructed.

Mother is not so clumsy. Respect for her sprouted.

Mother flagged something inside me: my fondness of quiet reading and writing would not contribute to the functioning of a small business. I would have to analyze, learn, and adapt to the new country.

My worst experience was Hurricane Josephine, 1996.

Musty air with hazy light rain brushed over my face, a chill in the early morning. Clad in my gabardine and galoshes, I sat upright in my neighbors' speedboat, steered by their son, Joe, a 17-year-old blonde boy.

We sliced the wind and misty drizzle, broke the currents to arrive at Lafreniere Park. Low land by Lake Pontchartrain, chimneys and roof lines vacillating on the ocean-like expanse.

Yellow kayaks, orange rescue boats dotted the black water. The local authority had evacuated my tenants in the lake-side house before this disaster.

We sailed along Esplanade Avenue to go home. Our houses, in the morning light, appeared bobbing on the receding water.

I got inside my house, took off my wet raincoat and rubber boots in the front foyer.

"Why did you go out so early? It is dangerous after the storm," said Antonio, my husband, in a distressed tone.

"Joe was out cruising on his motorboat, so I tagged along." I wiped my face with a towel. "Free rent for the double while I clean and repair. The six-plex and the commercial strip were fine." I poured water from the bottle into the saucepan on the butane camp stove to make coffee and to boil eggs.

"Thank God you are okay. Do not go out again. Wait till things are restored and the water subsides," Antonio said, stroking my back and kissing my damp hair.

"Those buildings were in my head since the storm started." I turned to face him as he fetched the eggs from the icebox; his usual air of authority had shed in the face of my furtive suffering.

It had been 12 years since I started our small business. I was sure he noticed my metamorphosis: first his lover, became his wife, then mother of his child. With the enterprise, strands of gray streaked my hair, fine lines gathered around my eyes. An innate, visceral self sprouted inside me. I had never experi-

Metamorphosis

enced this primeval surge of my inner being. My family had churned out educators and scholars for generations. We were studious, well-educated, polite, and refined. That was the woman Antonio married. Now a new me occupied that shell, ruthless in negotiating the prices of properties, merciless in parleying on interest rates, relentless in pursuing bargains. Scouted out migrant laborers by visits to Hispanic churches, studied Spanish from a cassette tape player when I drove.

Deep inside my darkest reservoir was a feral woman. She writhed out of her domestic bondage and returned to her wild state, became a sharp and savvy businesswoman, no longer the introverted book worm jailed in her study. I discarded my timeworn identity like dried up corn husk, embraced something new and precarious. I became a mixture of old-world intellect and new world adventuring.

I have my mother inside me. •

Copyright 2022, Catherine C. Con

Catherine C. Con, published in *Emrys Journal*, *Tint Journal*, *The Bare Life Review*, *The Petigru Review*, *HerStry*, *Shards*, *Emrys Journal Online*, *National Women's History Museum*, *Catfish Stew*, *Change Seven*, *Longridge Review*, *Limit Experience Journal*, *On The Run*, *Light House Weekly*, *New York Times*, *Black Fork Review*.

Nominated for 2020 PEN/Robert J. Dau Short Story Prize for Emerging Writers; selected for "2020 Local Authors" by Greenville County Library, SC. Finalist for the Anne C. Barnhill Prize for Creative Nonfiction. First place for Lighthouse Weekly March Fiction Contest. Serves presently on the Board of Directors, South Carolina Writers Association.

Poor James
by Mary Clements Fisher

I was afraid. Not of dying, though my brother's death conjured premonitions of my own. But of living with regrets. Flying from the coast, then driving through fallow fields dotted with stranded homesteads, I scanned the bleak horizon for fond memories of poor James.

Seventeen years younger, I hadn't grown up with James. I first viewed his life through Mama's lens. Her ghost still whispered in my ear. Having a *Grapes of Wrath* baby and raising my brother and sister solo during World War II, when Papa joined up, hardened Mama. Plus, James felt fatherless at age 10. Papa didn't come home for good until James turned 24.

Navy brats, we moved and moved again. James and my sister changed schools 13 times before finishing high school. Crossing the country three times his junior year, James missed studying the Civil War altogether. He'd joked once, "Geography was my strong subject." School offered solace to my sister and me. It delivered disappointment to poor James.

Mama sobbed when James flunked out of college. He stayed stoic and silent until I received a university scholarship.

Poor James

His "You'll just end up married" irritated me. I did marry, graduated, taught, and then turned businesswoman. One Christmas, I asked about his job at the oil station and his brood of four. He bristled. "Proud Mary, married to her career. Selfish, too, with one lonely child."

"How would you know anything about my work? Or how hard it was to have one precious baby." My eyes blazed with anger and hurt. He apologized. I didn't accept. Like children, we picked at scabs. Our scars faded only with age.

After that spat, we avoided discussions about family and fortunes and exchanged clipped chat about the weather and our health. For years, James ended each call with, "Older is better than the alternative." Until at 91, he asked, "Who are you?"

He no longer remembered his crybaby sister who overshadowed his senior year or the toddler who tugged on his shirt tail. Or recalled our whooping wild rides from the farm to the town pool on steamy summer afternoons. With his arms in the air, his knee on the steering wheel, we flew over hill after hill. Thin threads stitched our relationship together until it unraveled.

My last in-person visit, casting about for clarity and comfort, poor James declared my mom hadn't been his mother. My shock sank into sorrow.

"Aunt Vi was my real mother. She called me 'my little Jimmy.'"

I squeezed his hand. "Vi *did* love you. So did Mama, in her way." He frowned. I'd felt Mama's affection and acceptance. I ached he hadn't. Had he heard Mama, or me, call him "poor James"? Pity made a sour substitute for love. "*I* love you." He closed his cloudy eyes.

Missed opportunities and misunderstandings popped up mile after mile until I saw the sign: "Clarks, Population 363." James' hometown for 60 years. No pumps stood at the gas station where he'd worked. Boards covered the broken windows of the bank. But, in the distance, blue skies outlined the roof of his home—his place of pride.

No turning back, I parked in front of the VFW Hall. A flapping banner invited all to "James Clements' Celebration of Life." Taped to the open door, a collage poster pictured a laughing baby James, a handsome high school graduate, a dashing Army corporal, a jubilant bride and groom, proud parents with three sons and one daughter, and a glowing grandfather. I gaped at the happy faces.

I crept into a dim, empty room. Early or too late? Past the bar, past head shots of fallen veterans, past vending machines, his family—minus his wife Jane, dead last year—stood in a circle with heads bowed. I cleared my throat.

My niece waved me to join. "Does anyone have another memory to share?"

James' youngest son spoke. "Dad never met a stranger he didn't like. As teenagers, we rolled our eyes and muttered

Poor James

'WTF' when he hung around a half hour outside the grocery store visiting. We asked, 'Who was that guy?' Dad would say, 'Don't know, but a fascinating fellow.'" James fared better with strangers than with Mama or me.

One granddaughter added, "Grandpa loved Grandma Jane's sweet rolls."

Mama deemed Jane a pitiable choice. *No. Mama got that wrong.* I offered a too-long-forgotten memory.

"The spring I turned 12, James and Jane became engaged. Late at night, they giggled and whispered on our sofa at the bottom of the stairs while I crouched at the top and eavesdropped. Jane warbled, *'Oh, Jimmy'* as James wooed. I didn't get it then—James had found the love of his life."

At the gravesite, my heart at peace at last, I celebrated my brother Jimmy. •

Copyright 2022, Mary Clements Fisher

Mary Clements Fisher relished her careers as an educator and businesswoman and celebrates her current mother/grandmother, sweetheart, student, and writer status in Northern California. Writing makes sense of her mad and muddled moments. She published in *Quail Belle Magazine, Adanna Journal, Passager Journal, The Weekly Avocet,* Personal Story Publishing Project, *Prometheus Dreaming Journal,* and *The Closed Eye Open.* Join her @maryfisherwrites and https://maryfisherwrites.squarespace.com

Homeless in LA
by Jill Amber Chafin

"What now?" I asked as the airport crowd slowly dispersed.

Nobody wanted to say it: We had nowhere to go. My older brother, Jason, had nothing—no cash, no credit cards. Mom and Dad had $600. I had $1,500, plus a credit card with a $3,000 limit. My family promoted me to be their savior.

"I don't want to go back to Arizona," Mom said with a sigh. "Not after that big farewell party."

"Well, we have to go somewhere," Dad said. "We can't stay in LA."

"I've always wanted to go to college in Boulder, Colorado," I blurted.

"Uh, sure," Dad said, cleaning his glasses on his wrinkled T-shirt. "Why not?"

Mom and Jason shrugged. Dad led us to the rental car counters. At least we had a plan!

It turns out you must be over 21 to rent a car in America, and I, at 19, was the only one with a credit card. The woman behind the Budget counter raised her eyebrows, glancing at our tattered luggage and our sweat-stained clothes. Defeated, we dragged ourselves to a nearby row of plastic seats, sinking into them and propping our legs on our tower of suitcases.

"We have to buy a car," Dad finally said. "A car lot has to be nearby, right?"

Our nods were weary and heavy, our minds clouded with jetlag, hunger, and fear. I found an ATM and withdrew the daily limit—$1,000—and handed the crisp bills to Dad.

"Jason and I'll take a cab," he said. "We'll find something."

They disappeared into LA's early morning haze. Mom and I remained tethered to baggage claim #4, our agreed meeting spot—it was 1998, before cell phones and nonstop connectivity. I bought snacks, drinks, and random magazines, settling in.

Mom always believed everything works out when you follow a dream. She'd read about immigrating to New Zealand and thought it'd be easier to apply for visas and work permits once we arrived. We sold most of our belongings and flew away on a whim. However, the legal paperwork can take months to get approved. We'd debated laying low like refugees, waiting for visas that may never manifest, but the risk of deportation was too high.

"But Dad had that job offer…" Mom's voice cracked. Frantic travelers streamed past. Everyone in a hurry, everyone with a somewhere to go.

I obsessively checked the wall clock. Dad and Jason had been gone eight hours. Panic brewed in my gut. A loud announcement blared a warning about leaving your luggage unattended. *Don't worry*, I thought. *This luggage is all we got.*

Then the doors parted and LA spit Dad and Jason back to us, exhausted.

"We got a car," Jason announced.

"It only cost $1,200," Dad said. He heaved our suitcases onto the car's roof, securing them with rope and bungee cords.

We clambered in, *Grapes of Wrath* style. I nicknamed the dilapidated, rusty, burnt-red car Rosasharn. Dad turned the key, swearing. I prayed. Rosasharn gave a spurt and a shudder, and she lurched forward, chugging along with little hiccups.

Aspects of my family life growing up remained an enigma, like when we lived in a rustic log cabin without running water in Wisconsin, and how we moved cross country without jobs, and then again, to the other side of the world with barely enough money to cover the plane tickets. These contradictory moments were part of the adventure, all I'd ever known.

An hour later a reluctant Rosasharn ground to a halt at a Shell station. Dad popped the hood, steam hissed out. Then he slammed the hood shut. "We're spending the night here."
"In this parking lot?" I asked, in shock. disbelieving.
"Yup."
"What about dinner?" *Maybe a hotel?*
"I can't be bothered," Dad said.
"Look. There's a *Subway*." Jason pointed.

Homeless in LA

"You guys go," Mom said, stifling a sob. "We're not hungry."

Jason and I hurried across the parking lot. We ate in silence, crouched on the concrete still hot from the scorching day, then headed to our lodging for the night—Rosasharn. Dad's snores rattled throughout the car.

"Goodnight," Jason whispered.

"Night." I'd never spent the night in a car. The temperature and moisture from our breathing rose quickly, like sitting in a steamy sauna, or trapped in the bowels of hell.

I could've taken my cash and bought a plane ticket to wherever my heart desired. I could have gotten a job and found my own place. But I'd learned one sure thing in my 19 years of adventure and unexpected surprises—family sticks together, and we take turns being the savior.

I pulled out my cardigan, bunched it into a pillow, and leaned my head against the window. We were homeless and almost broke, but I was with my family. We'd figure it out in the morning. We always did. •

Copyright 2022, Jill Amber Chafin

Jill Amber Chafin is a personal finance writer for LendingTree, an aerial dance teacher, and a mother to two small children in Chapel Hill, North Carolina. She co-hosts a nation-wide writers' critique group where she teaches workshops on the craft of writing. Connect through Facebook group The Writers Inspirational Network (WIN). She is currently querying agents for her domestic novel while also working on a young adult novel and her memoir. This story is one of many unique adventures she shared with her eccentric family.

They Don't Leave Us
by Lorraine Martin Bennett

I had heard as a child the adage: *the dead do not die, not when you love them.* I did not believe it. Now I do. The departed souls of those we cherished do not leave us. They return in ways simple, profound, unexpected, and entirely unpredictable.

I first became aware of this after my grandmother passed and violets began to grow in my yard. My grandparents' house was the playground of my childhood. Their five children, including my dad, grew up in that house. Their grandchildren, including me, played on their long L-shaped front porch. We tried to touch our toes to the ceiling as we pushed their large porch swing higher and higher. Our twilight hours were spent chasing fireflies across their sycamore-shaded front yard.

In my grandmother's back yard each spring, violets patterned the ground with a mesmerizing carpet. Now in spring when I see violets with their purple and white heads nodding through the early grass, she is there, pointing her finger in excitement and chattering happily at their appearance.

My grandfather, who preceded my grandmother's going by
years, was straight and strong as an oak. I remember his low,
steady voice. I never heard him raise it but when he spoke,
people stopped whatever they were doing and listened.
His hands were large, gnarled, and capable. Now when I see an
oak, especially an ancient one with its hard and durable trunk,
its spreading and comforting canopy, its resilience to wind,
snow, sleet, rain, and hail, my grandfather comes to me as
strong and steadfast in my memory as that oak.

My flighty and frothy mother-in-law, a minister's widow, lived
with my husband and me for two decades. She cross-stitched
my dining room chair cushions, needlepointed my napkins,
and embroidered holiday runners for my Christmas table.
A very able church pianist, she often took to her upright
during evening hours to play the old hymns she loved so much.

Most of all, she adored butterflies. She fastened their
magnetized images across her refrigerator door. Today when
I see a bright, flickering flash in the sunlight, she is there,
and I can hear her laughter.

My own mother loved hummingbirds and anticipated their
arrival every spring. She loved to paint—birds, still life portraits
of fruits, vegetables, flowers, beautiful vistas. Over the years
her canvasses have covered my walls. She took note
of seasonal changes in ways I never could. Her artist's eye
observed emerging shifts in the colors of sky, grass, and leaves.
Each year as February's chill departed and new leaves made
their appearance on trees exhausted from winter's capri-
ciousness, she would comment on the various hues and

shadings of greens across her beloved Blue Ridge Mountains—from sage to olive to teal to emerald.

Now she comes to me in springtime, not with the hummingbirds but just when new leaves begin their long-anticipated entrance.

My husband, and soulmate, was an astute observer and writer of the Blue Ridge with its environmental glories and challenges. He wrote every other week in the newspaper of happenings around our area, including topics making him unpopular with certain readers. He was highly offended by a local group's efforts to develop cabins within the national forest and carve dirt roads through Forest Service lands. That topic alone fueled enough fury for a dozen columns.

But his newspaper musings also honored these storied mountains in other ways. From an author whose books he loved, the novelist and short story writer Louis L'Amour, he took the heading for his own column, *The Far Blue Mountains*.

Now when I am driving these mountain roads and crest a hilltop with the far blues waiting in the distance, my late husband is with me.

My father spent many hours of his life working a farm. Every spring, without fail, he carefully planted a large garden with potatoes, squash, cucumbers, tomatoes, okra, corn, green beans. He loved the mountains and the land and took particular notice of any changes in weather. He was quick to offer observations to anyone who would listen.

They Don't Leave Us

I have been waiting for my father to come in a breeze, a storm, a sudden gale, or in ripples of thunder and lightning. He has been gone for more than a dozen years. So far, he has not made an appearance, but of one thing I am certain:

He will. •

Copyright 2022, Lorraine Martin Bennett

Lorraine Martin Bennett is a print, web, and broadcast journalist who grew up in Murphy, North Carolina. After graduating from UNC-Chapel Hill, she began her career on the Atlanta Journal, writing features and covering news. She became the first woman to head a domestic bureau at the Los Angeles Times. She joined a fledgling CNN, completing her career at CNN International. She still practices her craft by copy editing and occasionally writing stories for the Clay County Progress weekly. Her first novel, a psychological thriller titled *Cat on a Black Moon*, is due to be published later this year.

Philadelphia to Wilson
by Ginny Foard

As he came down the aisle, his worn jeans sagged but held his waist firmly. His T-shirt was tucked in, a cap hid his eyes. A down jacket puffed out, fitting for October in Philadelphia. He was bow-legged. He slung a duffel bag overhead before sitting down.

The train pulled out carrying us, two strangers, south to lands of our heritage.

His billboard-sized phone's large icons gave away his age. He answered a call, sent text messages. Then he plugged in an earplug and sank into silence. Thank God I wouldn't have to listen to nonsense for hours on end.

Another phone call. "Tell me what it's doing," he said. "Remember I'm gone this weekend? I'll be down in Wilmington. ... See you next week. Wednesday? ... Bye-bye." He and his earplug leaned back. His eyes closed. His hands spread on his lap, the phone dark and silent.

Again. "Hello, Mr. Richards, ...Yes ... Well, I can't get there until next week. ... Fine, we can look at it then. ... Thank you, see you later." Emails arrived, he smiled at photographs, he typed. His earplug stayed on. He nodded, maybe asleep.

Then the train stopped. We sat, seeing a field, vast waving crops, no roads, no train stations. A deep Southern voice announced that a heat advisory warning meant the train must go slower on the hot tracks. We'd be late.

Beside me, he searched his phone and then asked, "Do you have to make a connection? You're going to Wilson too, aren't you? It's 97 degrees there."

"I'm getting off at Wilson. How much time do you have for your connection?"

He grimaced. "Twenty minutes. My nephew picks me up in Wilmington tonight. I can't miss the bus. I hope the bus stop is near the train; I haven't done this before."

"Let's find out." I fiddle with my phone.

He mused, "I'm helping my nephew paint my aunt's house. This heat's a worry, ... if I even get there. Usually, my family comes up to me. One of the kids lived with me for a while. I put him to work, made him follow rules. Once that got straight, we got along fine. ... I don't drive, I'm on disability. But I like working. I do handyman work. It makes me feel good and helps with the bills. ... The man who's calling me forgets we just talked, he'll call again soon. He's nice, but it wears me out. His son will check on him tonight, he knows I'm out of town."

"Is it hard, not driving?"

He tells me about his life and jobs. One person gave his name to another, now they all call him. Getting old means being tired, he said. He pays attention to his health and medicines. He grew up down south, started work there, then found better jobs and pay up north. His family visits. He smiles as he describes his children and their children, their talents and hobbies. On his phone, he shows me his grandson who he helped raise. One photo leads to another, church events, graduations, birthdays, the dress his daughter loves best, her smile.

And now, his elderly aunt's house is falling apart. He's brought his painting clothes to spend three days repainting it. They'll need every minute. He wants an on-time train.

I think about my family and Wilmington—the Queen Anne's house built by my great-grandfather, his family's 1889 first Thanksgiving dinner inside its unfinished frame, my grandmother's childhood home where she returned with four toddlers, including my father, after my grandfather's suicide. And down the road from her husband's grave was the house my grandmother moved into with her children. Generations of my family now rest in that cemetery, neighbors to each other.

I think of 1920s family photos. My dad and his siblings in Ida Lofton's arms, crying, laughing, arguing. Her thick circular bottle-glass spectacles glaring in reflected light. My 90-year-old father swore, "Ida was a saint." And "she was family," he

declared. Regretfully, shaking his head sadly, "We deviled her."
As was custom then, Ida lived "on the Black side of town."

I said nothing to my train companion of my family history. We knew two different Wilmingtons, two sides of town, two rivers of history. Our happenstance companionship bound us equally to the whims of trains and hot metal. History's divisions had no place here.

"Where are you eating tonight?" he asked.

"What's good in Wilson?"

"The truckers go to an old barbecue place, Parker's. You'd never look twice at it. Around back is the take-out line—there's always lines of people waiting. You can sit down family style, too. Let me tell you how to get there. ..."

I waved goodbye to his bus. It had waited for our train.

Supper at Parker's was marvelous. •

Copyright 2022, Ginny Foard

Ginny Foard visits all over while her mail stacks up in a post office box near family in South Carolina. She's curious about people and things. Southern upbringing taught her there are always interesting stories. And don't jump to believe the first thing you hear. Listen. Ask questions. Ponder. There's more to learn.

At 5 and 95, Mother Was a Star
by Arlene Mandell

Mother always told me she was born with a song in her heart. Her life proved this to be completely true. At 4, she was discovered to be a piano prodigy. At 5, she gave a recital at Carnegie Hall in Manhattan.

She also entered kindergarten at 5 and boasted later about how she was introduced on the first day of school: "This is my daughter, Helen. She plays piano." My mother was promptly drafted to play piano for the game musical chairs. The teacher lifted her onto the piano stool, and with her chubby little legs dangling down, she played children's songs while the other kids ran around the chairs. At the teacher's signal, the music stopped. Whoever had no chair was "out." Word spread and EVERYONE came to watch! Mother fretted about not running around with the others but loved her celebrity status as she became known.

Mother was advised, however, not to pursue a pianist's career—her hands were too small, they said. So, she married, raised me, and turned her passion to cooking. This delighted Dad who loved good food expertly prepared. Dad also loved show tunes and made sure to get us front-and-center seats

At 5 and 95, Mother Was a Star

at spectacular Broadway musicals. At home, Mother played his favorite songs on the piano, invariably ending with her favorite, *The House I Live In*, made famous by Frank Sinatra, starring in the movie of the same name.

In later years and while living in Florida, Dad's long illness depleted their nest egg; he agonized about Mother's future. I reassured him that my husband and I would care for Mom; but, secretly, panic set in! I had already filed for divorce and was rooming in a boarding house to escape a bad situation. I had not told my parents. I wanted Dad's passing to be peaceful. Transporting his body by plane from Florida to the gravesite in New York, plus memorial services in both places, wiped out their remaining savings.

After the funeral, I told Mother I'd move into the apartment with her and get a job--ASAP. With my salary and her Social Security check, we could make it work by living frugally, which we did, amicably, for years. A highlight of those years was inviting families with youngsters to come in for a "piano lesson." Mother sat with them on the piano bench, took their index fingers, and plunked out the Happy Birthday song. The children were thrilled; when we walked through the neighborhood, they'd rush over to hug her, shouting, "Helen! Helen!"

At 95, early dementia and a terrible fall landed Mother in the hospital. The doctor said she needed permanent, full-time care. We could not afford this; panic set in. Again! I would have to take care of her myself. Hungry to be an artist, I had been studying at night school. Dejected, I told my class why I was dropping out. An elderly classmate suggested discreetly I first visit a nearby nursing home. If I liked it, call her, she said; she knew the director and could put in a good word for Mother.

Visiting, I was impressed by their music-therapy program, but the cost was prohibitive; however, Mother was deemed eligible for Medicaid. Then a cantankerous married couple was transferred out, freeing up a two-bed, Medicaid-authorized room. They admitted Mother whose new roommate, Lucille, warmly welcomed her. Lucille was a fun-loving foodie of ample proportions. She lived to eat, and ingeniously connived to have taboo edibles smuggled in. The two became best buddies and, though wheelchair-bound, looked out for each other.

On Mother's first day in music group, she joined a circle of people keenly waiting as the therapist distributed maracas, cymbals, triangles, castanets, and tambourines. Mother got the big bass drum. She played with panache, ad-libbing rhythmic beats and showy flourishes while keeping perfect time to the recorded music. The therapist was flabbergasted! Word spread and EVERYONE came to watch! Mother boasted to me: "I'm a big celebrity here—I feel like a schoolgirl starting my life all over again." This was music to my ears after worrying about her adjustment.

When Mother passed, I donated her piano to the home; a plaque attached to it reads: "Helen's Piano." Returning to visit Mother's friends, I saw her piano had been placed in the dining room of the Alzheimer's Unit for the music therapist to play at mealtimes. It is their own sort of "Happy Hour." Even those with severe memory loss sing out intermittent snippets

At 5 and 95, Mother Was a Star

of songs buried so deep in memory, no disease could erase them. And as if Old Blue Eyes had ordained it just for Mother, music now fills the air at *the house she lived in.* It fills me, too. She is the song in my heart—and still the brightest star in my eyes. •

Copyright 2022, Arlene Mandell

Arlene Mandell is an artist living in Linville, North Carolina. Enjoy her colorful portraits at Carlton Gallery in Banner Elk. A native New Yorker, she taught in Manhattan's Head Start program, then joined a travel magazine in Miami, Florida, where she met Captain Dan. Their relocation to the Blue Ridge Mountains inspired a love of writing. Her memoirs "Eye of the Dolphin," "Artist Borne," "Gobsmacked in the Gulfstream," "Renegade Daughter," "It Started with a Typo," "Shopping for the Homeless," "Thirteen Candles in the Dark," and "The Promise of Romance" appear on "6-minute Stories" podcast.

The Tattoo
by Brooke Dupree

It was skate night for my daughter's 4th grade class and since it was close to Halloween, the kids were encouraged to dress up. Travis, my husband, took pictures of Caroline donning her new llama costume at the skating rink door.

When we stepped inside, the smell of old metal and stale popcorn hit my nose, taking me back to my own skating days. We saw only a few tables, the old kind typical of skating rinks, with wooden bench seats curved around both sides of the table. We stood, watching Caroline on the rink with her rented skates, holding on to the rail. Although nervous, she soon spotted a few classmates. Other parents also loitered about, chatting, taking pictures. This wasn't my scene. I hated school functions (still do), but "parenting," right?

We looked for a place to sit. Travis noticed two women at a four-person table; he asked if we could join them. "Oh sure," said the dark-haired woman on the end. We sat, uncomfortably, opposite them.

After light introductions, Melissa, we learned, was there with her children. Our backgrounds were similar, and she was as wary of school functions as I was. As we spoke, Melissa noticed my artistic *Type 1 Diabetic* tattoo on my right wrist. It's meant to catch the attention of medical emergency personnel should they find me unconscious. She asked politely if I was "Type 1," the common phrase used among fellow diabetics, mostly to differentiate "Type 1s" from the "Type 2s," whose diseases are different.

"Yes, for almost 30 years," I said, glancing at my wrist.
I was leery at the prospect of having to describe my disease to a stranger.

To me, my diabetes was like a neighbor's barking dog: we didn't get along. Even though I knew it well, I had no control over its constant noise making. By the time I turned 35, I'd had my share of surgeries on my eyes, hands, and fingers and began experiencing the first stages of gastroparesis, paralysis of the nerves of the stomach lining, which would have meant a lifelong feeding tube. Literally, this disease was getting on my nerves. But the daily struggle of controlling diabetes for three decades was mentally draining: glucose monitoring, insulin boluses, and unpredictable episodes of high and low blood sugar had taken their toll and spawned bouts of depression and wretched mood swings.

Melissa told us that her husband "*had* Type 1." Of course, I took this to mean past tense, and offered my condolences.

"Oh no," she said smiling, "he had a pancreas transplant about eight years ago. No more diabetes."

What? I thought. I felt slightly numb. I asked Melissa to repeat that bit about the "pancreas transplant." I wasn't sure I heard that right.

Melissa explained that her husband had a new pancreas from a donor, and basically, the diabetes was—*poof*—gone.

The concept of being diabetes-free rattled me. Skeptical, I quizzed Melissa intensely. She patiently answered, while Travis mostly listened and googled about what she said. We exchanged phone numbers.

When skate night ended, the dusty parking lot was dark. Other parents were leaving as well, headlights skimming over the other cars, beaming toward the road. Perched in the front seat, I thought, *Unbelievable.* I felt betrayed by my many doctors and specialists over the years. I'd despised doctor's visits—they filled my schedule and drained my bank account. Good news from my physicians was rare and often consisted of scolding and finger pointing. Diabetes was the reason I was the outcast in middle school, why Caroline's birth was difficult, the cause of a lot of life-long turmoil.

I asked Travis, "Do you think I should—?"

And before I could finish, he interrupted, "Yes, yes, I think you should at least look into it."

"But—?"

"All you can do is ask. We will figure out the rest."

The Tattoo

So, I did not see it then, the serendipitous meeting with Melissa in a skating rink where I did not want to be, and especially since I'd spent most of my life trying to hide my T1D. The inked words on my wrist were just one of many tattoos I have. But this one was the only one I did not, and could not, cover up. I'd barely had it a year before that night. It wasn't until eight months later, after my own pancreas transplant, and being diabetes-free, that I would realize the unexpected gift that cursive, scrolly tattoo would provide me.

I no longer have Type 1 diabetes. Blood sugar monitoring and insulin injections have been replaced with a simple medication regimen. I no longer deal with diabetes pain—legs, eyes, or mental drainage from the worry over highs and lows.
The tattoo, however, is still there. I have considered getting it re-done, but then a stranger will point it out—"You have Type 1?"

"Actually," I say, "I *had* diabetes." •

Copyright 2022, Brooke Dupree

Brooke Dupree earned a BA in English from the University of South Carolina, an MA in Writing from Coastal Carolina University, and an MFA in Creative Writing from Queens University. Her personal essay, "All the Leaving Times," can be found in *SOREN Lit* magazine. When she is not dutifully working on her memoir or sharing the parenting tasks of a teenage daughter, Brooke can be found teaching English composition at one of the local colleges or universities in the Greenville, South Carolina area. Brooke loves to read, travel, and tell stories.

Grabbing for the American Dream
by Akira Odani

Basketball in a Tokyo high school was my outlet to release the rage I felt against my father. Towering an inch or two over the other boys, and grinning with superiority, I caught the ball and scored often. We practiced on a dirt court. The yellowish powder colored my black hair blond and painted arms and legs with sweat streaks. My mother lamented my dirty appearance but could not afford firewood to heat bathwater nor give me a couple of dimes to visit the public bathhouse. I splashed icy water on my face and neck at the kitchen sink, thoroughly unsatisfied.

My father was a middle-aged spoiled brat. He pursued dubious get-rich-quick schemes and squandered what he had inherited. He shunned our home, hiding from creditors for days and weeks. A coward, he appeared only when he was safe from the eyes of the mean-looking, tattooed thugs hired by the loan sharks to get their money. Fortunately, my mother maintained a modest flower shop attached to our living quarters to spare her family of four children from starving.

One autumn afternoon in the flower shop, Mom clipped stems of roses and changed the water in tin cans while asking me about the afternoon game. As the sun descended low over the roofs of nearby homes, a glaring beam of light shot through the large glass window of the store. A figure dressed in a dark suit emerged out of nowhere at the doorstep, his face indistinguishable because of the light shining behind him. I recognized him, my father, before my mother did. He slipped by us without even a hello, reached the cash register and grabbed the money. I cringed.

"No! Hiro. That's for the inventory and our food." Mom jumped and seized the sleeves of his jacket. He brushed her arms aside, grunting like a bulldog. With Yen bills in his pocket, he left the shop, slithering away like a venomous snake. I stood with my mouth open. No words came out nor could I process what had happened. Mom collapsed on a nearby stool, weeping, "I can't do this, Akira. It is SO hard!"

Unable to intervene, I had witnessed yet another abuse against my mother committed by my father. Later that evening, my siblings and I shared a measly bowl of steamed rice with two raw eggs cracked on it, dribbled with soy sauce. We ate supper as if at a funeral. My mother did not eat.

Scratching my itchy skin and oily hair, I yearned for a bath. Hunger worsened my adolescent angst. On meandering walks, I kicked pebbles just to feel alive. I bicycled aimlessly at frantic speeds. *What's going to happen to me? Is my college education doomed?* My other choices were assembly-line laborer, noodle-shop cook, and dishwasher.

At the bottom of my despair, I found wisdom that said my life's destiny was mine to choose. Blaming others helped no one. I could not pick a different father, but I could change the situation where I wrote my next chapter. The United States of America stood up as the shiny candidate for my future destination. The appeal of the American dream had seeped into my head through images in *Life* magazine and through the movie *West Side Story*. Most Japanese viewed Americans as the saviors of our self-inflicted wartime miseries. Even my mother, who lost her father and her first child to the firebombing in 1945, never objected to my desire. She encouraged me to follow this unusual path I chose.

I earned "A's" in high school English and devoured advanced classes offered by elite instructors. The Far East Network, the radio station for the American soldiers in Asia, became my favorite source of music and newscasts. Seeking opportunities to practice my language skills, I sought out random American tourists and soldiers downtown. "Hi, there. Can I help you? I speak some English." Many allowed me to be their temporary city guide. My reward was their amused smiles.

An American-inspired liberal arts college in Tokyo offered me additional English training. Within two years, I became a professional interpreter. I earned my living through the assignments and eventually I obtained a scholarship from Rotary International to attend Brown University for a graduate degree.

Settling later in New York, I launched my marketing and consulting firm and helped American businesses locate partners and investors in Japan and vice versa. After I retired, a small college in New York offered me a teaching opportunity. I happily grabbed it as a way to repay my debt to numerous American benefactors.

My father could not provide what I needed. But his failure was the catalyst which propelled me to seek my own destiny, to grab for a new dream in a new country.

For that, I am grateful. •

Copyright 2022, Akira Odani

Akira Odani lives in the ancient city of St. Augustine, Florida. He is a member of the Taste Life Twice Writers' group. Born in Tokyo, he wrote extensively in the past for the Japanese media, but more recently his interest has turned to writing in English and on subjects that intersect the cultural and social characteristics of the two peoples. Some of his work has appeared in the pages of anthologies sponsored by the Florida Writers Association. He stays active, meditating, swimming, and playing pickleball.

Editor's note: Akira Odani served as a simultaneous interpreter for U.S. Presidents Jimmy Carter and Ronald Reagan.

The Power Drill
by Lynne E Williams

I teeter atop a plastic stepstool on my new apartment's little patio, choking back hiccupy shrieks of frustration. The power drill in my hand epitomizes my many failures. Each buzzy scratchy whir invokes a shortcoming.

Zhirrrrrr! Failure to reach my potential, or even reach *for* my potential. I'm a musician, an actor, a writer, meant to be leaving my mark on the world. But instead of chasing my dreams, I'm doing phone support for Microsoft, a soul-sucking, stressful job that doesn't leave time for much else. I don't even *like* computers.

Shirrrrrr! Failure to hold onto a relationship. Four fraught years is my new record. None of my previous relationships lasted even one.

Bzzrrrrrr! Failure to become a functional adult. At 31, I should have managed *that much*, at least. I have a full-time job, a car, an apartment. I pay my bills, do the dishes, empty the trash. Yet I still feel like an imposter, a lost little girl playing make-believe.

Tears and sweat salt my cheeks. Humidity-tightened curls poke at my eyes and stick to my face. Brushing them aside, I glare up at the spot where I envisioned a hook to hang a plant from, like the flowers and ferns that decorated my last place. Instead, there is just an ugly raw dent in the wooden ceiling beam where I've jammed the drill against it again and again, willing there to be a hole where my fancy new power tool flat-out refuses to put one.

The drill was an impulse purchase last week, after I moved out of the apartment we had shared. The impulse was of the "I'll show HIM I can live without him and his manly drill skills" variety. To prove, by way of owning power tools, that I actually *can* be a functional adult.

"Do you think you'd be happier with somebody else?"

I had asked the question over Kraft mac & cheese on a tense Saturday afternoon, fully expecting him to say "No, of course not!" Then we'd both smile-sigh with relief, say things to clear the air, and go back to falling asleep close together, ankles entwined, instead of coiled up on opposite sides, facing away.

His perfunctory "Yes" gutted me.

I had followed him from Massachusetts to Charlotte three years earlier, believing he was my future. We talked marriage. We named hypothetical children.

I left behind everything else that mattered to me: my parents, whom I had just begun unpacking from the carefully labeled "Mom" and "Dad" boxes I'd kept them in throughout childhood and adolescence; my best friend and soul twin, who is like the other half of me. I gave up my second-chair seat in the American Band wind ensemble, as much a part of me as I was of it.

I left behind my family's property in Vermont, where our 30-foot waterfall cascades down a postcard-picturesque gorge. Time stands still there; with an indefinable wonder I've only ever felt in *that* place.

All these things, and so much more.
For him, I gave up *home*.

He was *supposed* to say *no*.

Now my cat (no longer *our* cat) watches through narrowed eyes from across the living room, a safe distance from the open patio door. Tail atwitch, she oscillates between curiosity and alarm each time I run the drill. Its unfamiliar noise and my shrieky crying obviously irritate her sensitive ears and tender nerves. She isn't used to this place yet either.

I croak out a tearful "Aww, Moe, good puss-puss, you're ok" before shifting my attention back to the seemingly useless power tool in my hands. An all-too familiar "You suck at everything just give it up!" chorus in my head triggers a fresh round of tears, baptizing the drill.

Then, through the haze of wetness, I see it. A reverse setting on the drill's power switch, which is what the switch was set to!

The Power Drill

REVERSE! Who knew that a power drill had a *reverse*?

My sobs give way to near-hysterical giggles that push my cat over the edge. She scurries away to cower in the jumble of partly unpacked boxes by my bed.

Within minutes I have drilled the hole, twisted in the plastic-coated metal hook, and hung my new pot of dangling flowers. They cascade toward the floor like a fragrant waterfall of purple and pink happiness. I swipe away the last of my tears and stand firm on the patio, gazing up at my handiwork. A smile plays around my edges, reflecting a shift. My switch has been flipped to forward. I am barely aware of it, couldn't have named it, but there it is.

In that moment, for at least that moment, I am a functional adult. •

Copyright 2022, Lynne E Wiilliams

Lynne E Williams is a native New Englander who still wakes up every day a bit surprised to find herself in North Carolina. Lynne currently lives in Charlotte with her two cats, two dogs, two sons and their dad. She is an active member of Charlotte Writer's Club and a 2022 finalist in the club's non-fiction contest.

Our Wedding Plan
by Vicki Easterly

It was a happy time. Tom and I had been together for five years, and we had decided to marry. He gave me an antique diamond ring. I bought a long ivory shantung skirt with matching beaded top for the ceremony. My sister purchased her teal maid of honor dress and my nieces their purple one-strap bridesmaid's gowns. The wedding was set for January 1999.

That December 18, 1998, was a dreadfully dreary Friday. I still recall that because it was the day we found out.

My office on Broadway in Frankfort, Kentucky, was in the front of my home. I was taking a mid-morning break back in the kitchen, chatting with my secretary, Lisa, when Tom walked in. This was odd because his office was over on Main Street, where he should have been at that time of day.

He asked Lisa if we could have some privacy, then he sat down with me at the old oak table. For the first time, he told me he had been coughing up blood the past few weeks and he had x-rays the past week. He had been to the doctor that morning, he began, and had been told he had lung cancer, Stage IV. It had already spread to his adrenal gland. Calmly, almost detached, he shared that devastating news.

Because of his composure, it took a moment for this new reality to set in. The cancer was inoperable. The doctor had no treatment to recommend and gently had told Tom to go home and live out the time he had left, an estimated eight months. I felt like someone had hit me in the chest and knocked out my breath. I did not cry; I could not cry.

Tom wanted first to visit his dad, who was buried on a hill in the Lebanon Baptist Church Cemetery. We drove there and stood with a freezing wind attacking us as he "talked" to his father. Next, we went to his mother's house, where he began by saying he had some bad news. "Oh, I hope it ain't cancer!" she seemed to beg. It was cancer. She cried; I still did not.

I don't remember much about the rest of that day, except that we decided to move our wedding to the coming Sunday, only two days away. He first offered me an out from the marriage. I told him if I were going to love him "in sickness and in health, till death do us part" two weeks from then, I meant it all the more urgently two days away. Because Tom was an attorney, we were able to get into the courthouse on Saturday to obtain our marriage license. We had no engraved wedding invitations. All day we phoned friends and invited them to our "shotgun" wedding.

And so, we were married at 2 o'clock on December 20, 1998, in the Crestwood Baptist Church. Folks came with heavy hearts, but Tom would have none of that. "Today is to be a happy day—a happy day for Vicki," he declared.

We had no time to decorate, but the church had been decorated for Christmas with a large mural of Bethlehem and a brilliant display of red poinsettias. Because we had no time for a cake, my son and his wife offered us the top from their wedding cake from the year before, with the frozen-in-time plastic bride-and-groom figures still standing. It was too late for a florist, so my sweet sister drove to our farm and picked me the most precious bouquet of greenery, mistletoe, and dark red berries. She also sang, beautifully, a song I had written for the wedding. My white satin shoes were not yet dyed, so I wore them slightly "off color." None of those things mattered.

Finding a venue for a reception in two days was out of the question. But Tom's best friend and his wife, who lived in a beautiful horse-country mansion, gave us a reception as a wedding gift. They stayed up all Saturday night decorating their home and preparing a feast for us. Someone—I still don't know who—ordered a limousine to take us there. A glittering tall tree, shiny silver, and a scrumptious spread of delectables greeted us when we walked in the door. A special toast with Dom Perignon was proposed—not for health, but for joy. And joy we had. We celebrated our union into the night with our dearest friends and family.

Our Wedding Plan

That was our day, bittersweet, but more blessed and beautiful in its circumstances, one of the most special days of my life, not as we had planned, but as it was—just as it had to be.

By grace, we had two-and-a-half years together—until death did us part. •

Copyright 2022, Vicki Easterly

Vicki Easterly is a retired disability advocate, living in Frankfort, Kentucky, where she is a member of the Bluegrass Writers Coalition and the Society of Children's Book Writers and Illustrators. Her short story, "Hallie Holcomb's Hollow," was published by the UK Carnegie Press. Three of her memoirs are included in the Personal Story Publishing Project anthologies. Her first book, *Miracles in the Mundane*, was selected for inclusion in the annual Kentucky Book Festival. She currently is writing children's stories, memoirs, and poetry. She enjoys playing with her granddaughters and acting in community theatre.

A Soldier's Choice
by Lubrina Burton

From the driver's seat of my buddy Low's old 1980-something BMW, I squint up at the German traffic light, waiting for it to change from red to amber to green. Ancient stucco and half-timbered buildings surround me and drape lazy blooms from their window boxes.

The sun streams through the narrow corridor of shops and breweries to concentrate its energy on me where I sit behind the wheel. My Army fatigues have melted onto every square inch of my skin. I smell the failure of both my deodorant and this plan. With my right hand, I grip the shifter. As soon as the light turns amber, I will shift into first gear. When the light turns green, I will take my foot off the brake, gas it through the intersection, then move into second, third, maybe even fourth, barreling straight down the street to retrieve my friend. My left hand, though, sits poised to flip the lever of the turn signal. I'd make a right and hightail it back to base without him should my mind change along with the light.

"No Man Left Behind" is a commandment the Army has inscribed somewhere on stone tablets. Another rule, this one etched into our brains, "Thou Shalt Report Ten Minutes Prior," holds equal sway. When these directives conflict, our leaders have given us no guidance on what to do. Today I find myself in this dilemma. My buddy is MIA in town. Missing-in-action, gone, vanished, disappeared after our so-simple-it-cannot-fail plan to pay a cell phone bill is turning into a scheme doomed to fall apart. No one gets out alive.

I admit Bavaria in the new millennium may not be a hotbed of military conflict and Low has not dashed over no-man's-land into enemy fire. These facts do not mean our young lives—his by intention and mine by association—are in any less danger. If I cannot find my buddy and get back to base in time to report, then depending on our platoon sergeant's mood, which shifts with the winds, he can either understand our predicament or go as far as reporting us AWOL. Punishment for being absent without leave could range from mowing grass after duty to being dragged off by the Military Police.

"It won't even take that long," Low said to me with more hope than confidence. "We'll be back to base before lunch is even over." When he came looking for a friend, a driver, he swore he had the times and locations all mapped out. In a European town born during medieval times and designed for horse-drawn wagons, not motorized vehicles, parking is a problem along the cobblestone streets. He needed someone to drop him off while he ran into the T-Mobile shop to pay his bill, circle the block, then pick him up.

As we neared the phone store just moments ago, we saw women in strappy dresses and men in short-sleeved shirts gathered outside. The line of people stretched down the block and around the corner. Payday for German civilians and U.S. military must have been the same day. Clutching their phone bills, those in the growing line waved the papers in front of their faces in futile attempts to fan away the stagnant June air.

"Just slow down next to the curb," Low had said. "You don't even have to stop." He opened the passenger side door and did a combat roll into the street. I sped off, and from the rearview mirror, I saw him disappear into the crowd.

Now alone in the car, I tap the steering wheel, willing the light to change. Locals sip coffee at sidewalk cafes and bicyclists ride with fresh loaves in their baskets, while Volkswagen and Peugeot hatchbacks clog the street. Perched high on a steeple, a clock chimes its warning. If only I could move those hands back and change time. Perhaps, I would say "no" when my friend asked for help.

But I remember how a few months ago I arrived here alone, a soldier in a strange land. Low offered to help me navigate this new world. He helped someone struggling to find where she belonged in the Army, in a foreign country. He became a comrade, then a brother.

The sun has begun its retreat from its position high in the noon sky and a cool breeze gusts through the car's open

A Soldier's Choice

windows. The light changes from amber to green. My foot is on the gas, and I am already in gear. In front of me traffic parts. What perils still lie in wait, I do not know, but I see clearly now the path I will take. •

Copyright 2022, Lubrina Burton

Lubrina Burton lives in Lexington, Kentucky with her husband and pug, Lucy. She earned both her Psychology degree and post-baccalaureate certificate in Paralegal Science from Eastern Kentucky University. She is an alumnus of the Carnegie Center in Lexington, where she discovered a network of friends and fellow writers. Her work is featured in The Personal Story Publishing Project anthologies, *That Southern Thing*, *Trouble*, and *Curious Stuff*. Currently she is working on a memoir about her time in Europe with a pre-9/11 United States Army.

The Hounds of Antigua
by Wayne A. Barnes

In 2004, I spent seven glorious months on the Caribbean island of Antigua—*Mon*—investigating massive construction fraud at a dozen jobsites. I was a recently retired FBI agent and looked forward to investigating on an exotic island.

Each Monday morning, site managers reported large amounts of building material had disappeared from their projects, over months, totaling millions in theft. When the investigation was over, I had located 28 houses and an 8-unit apartment building, all built with stolen material. The thieves were those same managers.

During the investigation, I stayed at the *Blue Waters*, a splendiferous resort with fine breakfast cuisine that made me feel guilty if I did not jog beforehand.

A winding road took me up a hill that overlooked the sea. On the right, fenced land sloped up to magnificent houses. I would jog the route each morning, then return for a scrumptious meal.

As I jogged down the road, at a certain point off to the right, would come a cacophony of snarling and growling. A tall chain-link fence held back two large mongrels. Slow-moving cars would swerve away in surprise, and school children crossed to the far side of the street in fear.

In Antigua, as in many places, dogs are not house pets and have no names. Most are ferocious, like these two. One was a German Shepherd mix, and the other, a black Lab. Both had vicious streaks and impressive shoulder strength—think "Hounds of the Baskervilles."

Several of the diamond-shapes in the chain-link fence had been forced into circles by the dogs' thrusting snouts, their flesh rubbed raw.

Back home in San Diego, our family had raised Golden Retrievers, the most kid-loving dogs on the planet. Cirrus and Haley produced a litter that was featured on our annual Christmas letter with a cute puppy in each child's lap.

Now in Antigua, I called out to the angry dogs in my most inviting voice, "Cirrus, Haley—Cirrus, Haley." I gave a three-tweet whistle, how I used to call our Goldens down the beach. Here, the response was—*Nutin', Mon!* Didn't faze them at all.

The next morning, I brought a napkin filled with breakfast ham. I kneeled down to their frenzy, their snouts jabbing at me.

I tossed the meat over the fence. At first, they ignored it, but the wafting aroma got their attention. They stopped snarling long enough to gobble down the treat, then went back to growling. *OK,* I thought, *nice try.*

The next day was the same, but with more ham. Approaching the fence, I did the three-tweet whistle, and down the hill they charged.

"Cirrus! Haley! Ciiiir-rus! Haaaa-ley!" I called out, pleasantly. They just kicked up the dust and wolfed down the meat.

The next day, I did not toss the ham over the fence, but held it at their snouts, giving them a good whiff. I whistled and called their names. I risked my fingers and pushed the ham through the fence. This time, when the meat was gone, no anger, just searching for more, even whimpering. That was when I knew I had them. "Good boy, Cirrus! Good girl, Haley!" Off I jogged.

From then on, when I whistled, they came barreling down the hill, a slap-happy loping for their morning treat. I put my fingers through the fence, lovingly rubbing their necks and ears.

A few months into my investigation, I had to interview a doctor. When I saw the address, I had my suspicions.

After the interview, I admired the spectacular view and asked to step out on the patio. He suggested I not, as his dangerous dogs would tear me apart. I said I usually got along with animals and slid the door open. The doctor was terrified for me, having trained his feral dogs to attack.

I whistled. In a flash, his two "ferocious hounds" transformed into loving pets that rubbed against me as I scratched their ears. The doctor was astonished and baffled. I never let on how I had managed to be so loved.

The Hounds of Antigua

Five months after my case was over, I returned to Antigua with my family on their Easter break.

After breakfast, I packed up some ham and told my children, "I have a surprise. 'Cirrus and Haley' are right down the road." They couldn't imagine what I was talking about but got into the car.

I parked across from the fence, and two mongrels began their downward charge. I gave the three-tweet whistle and called out their names. In seconds, they were romping down the hill and happily barking.

My kids piled out of the car, and I gave them all ham to pass through the fence. My children's voices were all laughter and, I'll admit, I had tears in my eyes.

When I travel and want it to feel like home, I find a dog to welcome me—sometimes two! •

Copyright 2022, Wayne A. Barnes

Wayne A. Barnes was an FBI agent for 29 years, working Counterintelligence, Healthcare Fraud, and federal judicial backgrounds. He was a Black Panther in one undercover assignment. He has expertise in signatures, for personality analysis and forgeries. He first wrote true-spy stories debriefing intelligence defectors during the Cold War. His Bureau life and raising five children were fertile ground for a post-retirement writing career, having authored over 100 essays and three, as-yet unpublished books. He lives in South Florida and investigates privately, worldwide. For more of Wayne's essays, see: www.WayneBarnesWriting.com

Flooded
by Tara Thompson

I had no intention of dying that day—26, bald, hooked up to machines. Even as a child, fascinated by graveyards and ornate headstones, I'd visualized my death numerous times (the drama, the casket, the final words), and it had never, not once, looked like this.

I can't remember the exact moment my lungs flooded. It happened so quickly. A "STAT" order boomed over the intercom. Someone shoved a tube down my throat.

What I do remember is waking up in a daze, unable to speak. A doctor stood over me; medical staff swarmed like bees; and then I passed out. When I awoke, my right arm was strapped down to some type of board. I struggled against it. My pulse quickened.

I can't move.
I can't breathe.

A needle shot up a vein in my trapped hand. A catheter snaked through my urinary tract. Another catheter, sewn into my chest, dispersed chemo and drugs and blood transfusions, sometimes at the same time. This was the protocol for someone like me.

Leukemia.
Undergoing a bone marrow transplant from a donor.

I opened my mouth to ask, "What's happening?" but nothing came out. That was the worst part; that and the confusion. I tried again. Nothing. I motioned frantically with my left hand.

Trapped!

The nurse, who I later learned wasn't allowed to leave me until another nurse took over—*she's one of the dying ones*—tried to explain. "You're on a ventilator," she said. "There were some complications. Try to relax."

What I did not know was that my family had already been contacted and told that I might not make it, so they should come immediately.

My sister, who was my donor, perched on a metal chair by my side, clutching my free hand. My dad, who hovered nearby, gave me a red pen and yellow legal pad that he carried around during those endless hospital days. "It's okay, Hon," he said. His normally strong voice wavered.

I scribbled questions with my left hand. My dad and the nurse answered them when they could decipher my hieroglyphic scrawls. Years later, I found this pad and was startled seeing how much the ink resembled blood.

"Your lungs flooded," a nurse said.

"With marrow?" I wrote.
"No, with IV fluids. It's very unusual."
"Did the transplant work?"
"We don't know yet."

I couldn't write fast enough. *I'm running out of time; I don't have enough time.* This feeling would persist for years to come. At one point I threw the red pen across the room. It struck the wall with a loud thud and made my sister jump.

As the youngest patient to undergo the highly risky, adult bone marrow transplant in that hospital at that time, I had so much promise. My sister was a "perfect" match; I'd done "very well" with the chemo and radiation. What that means I don't know since I threw up all the time. I had trudged through hallway walks, pulling my pump, the nurses cheering me on; I'd blown into my plastic contraption to keep my lungs from collapsing. Yet, here I was, stuck on a ventilator. Was I a failure? *Just hang on one more day,* I told myself, over and over.

But the bigger question kept recurring: *Am I going to die?*

I don't recall when they took me off the ventilator. That's something I would like to remember, to celebrate even. But there was more to come—nearly two more months in semi-isolation with numerous bumps in the road.

I sometimes wonder why I made it off the soulless machinery and back into the world, with its rays of sunshine and fresh air. My dad would say it was positive thinking. "Think positive and do your best," he'd advise before piano recitals and exams. My mother would say it was God. And while I've always

Flooded

believed in God, I also saw too many people on my hospital floor who did not make it out, their lifeless bodies wheeled by my door as the nurses spoke in hushed tones: *Shhh, don't let the others know. It's bad for morale.*

The guy in the room beside me, who played his guitar to keep his spirits high, whose mouth sores were worse than mine: dead. The young girl I exchanged letters with, both of us with slick bald heads: dead. I'm sure their families prayed and thought positive thoughts. Where was God for them? There's no sense in any of it.

As my sister wheeled me through the hospital doors, I inhaled the crisp outside air for the first time in nearly three months and felt my lungs expand, like a butterfly taking flight. I had never seen or felt the world like this before. I was flooded with gratitude.

I survived.
I live. •

Copyright 2022, Tara Thompson

Tara Thompson lives in Durham, North Carolina. She holds an MFA in Creative Writing from the University of North Carolina Wilmington and was selected as a winner of the annual Piccolo Spoleto Fiction Open. Her short stories and essays have been published in *Wilma* magazine, *Charleston City Paper*, *The Square Table*, *Prick of the Spindle*, and more. This current essay is inspired by Tara's soon-to-be finished memoir, which is about her endless fight to survive cancer. Tara is also completing a contemporary novel.

All Things Considered
by Lois Elizabeth Hicks with Rudy Hicks

My son, Rudy, says he remembers the chilly Friday evening, October 11th, 1996. He left Siler City, North Carolina, to drive to Silk Hope over isolated country roads to retrieve Casper, his white mongrel pup, from the dog sitter.

He says he does not like to remember drinking *Old Grand-Dad* bourbon, downing enough to put him over the legal limit to drive. He remembers driving anyway, knowing but ignoring his impairment, then failing to turn with a curve on Jesse Bridges Road, and the Chevrolet Citation collapsing against an oak tree that stood beside the road.

Well, that wasn't so bad, he thought. But when he tried to push his body upright, he could not move.

When emergency personnel took him to Chatham Hospital in Siler City, where he worked as an admittance clerk and social work intern, he muttered, "need steroids," because he recognized his spinal cord injury. He remembers the subsequent helicopter airlift to Memorial Hospital in Chapel Hill.

Rudy remembers that post surgery the neurosurgeon approached his bed holding a transparent plastic vial that rattled when shook, and when the doctor poured the contents onto a bedside table, bone fragments rolled out like dice. Rudy remembers him saying, "You are quadriplegic."

Rudy rejected the diagnosis and believed that if he used his brain, he could make his limbs work. But instead of his mind overpowering his paralyzed extremities, it entered into a confused mix of hallucinations and dreams. He looked forward to sleep, hoping to dream of walking, of moving his body. When awake, he told in his whispering, gasping voice how he could accomplish impossible feats, how he climbed down from his hospital bed and, pulling oxygen hose and intravenous lines behind him, walked across the room to view his gaunt visage in a mirror.

No one could convince him that such a thing was impossible until the neurosurgeon returned to Rudy's bedside, declaring, "You have trouble accepting your condition."

The surgeon pulled a paper towel from the holder, sketched, slashed, explained: "Your paralysis is permanent." Then Rudy knew it was impossible to have walked or used his hands.

But if he accepted the doctor's prognosis, Rudy had to face his future. Every glimpse of that future filled him with despair, left him frightened, grieved, angry that he had done this to himself, had thought it okay to drive with his bloodstream infused with alcohol.

Rudy remembers his transfer to physical rehabilitation and learning to do new things. He remembers the first time he moved his right shoulder to move his upper arm, the first time he used a pencil stuck into a hand brace to turn pages of a book. He remembers learning how to feed himself a cheeseburger.

For the first time, Rudy dreamed he was in a wheelchair. He dreamed that he controlled the chair with a joystick and drove so fast that the chair lifted off the floor and flew. He found hope in that dream.

Rudy did not expect to live long with his damaged body. But it is now over 25 years later, years of physical pain, pressure sores, surgeries, years of knowing that one bad choice wrecked his life. He remembers but he does not dwell on the past. He is too busy getting through his day.

At 8:00 a.m. Rudy clicks the remote to unlock his door for an aide to enter and to allow Maggie, the black Labrador sleeping beside his bed, to go outside to relieve herself. He reviews his plans for the day. He will spend two hours directing the aide in completing his personal care and the various tasks necessary to put him in his power chair for the day.

He reviews the tasks for which he is responsible to share in keeping the household going with his parents, reminding them of appointments, then placing online orders for medical and household supplies.

After the morning aide leaves for the day, Rudy will take a slow wheelchair ride outdoors to allow Maggie to chase a rabbit or to sniff out the neighborhood or to tease a feral cat.

After lunch, at one o'clock, Rudy and Maggie will load into the Dodge van with a wheelchair ramp. A hired driver will carry them east on US Highway 64 to keep a medical appointment at Memorial Hospital in Chapel Hill.

When he returns from Chapel Hill, Rudy and Maggie will again explore the outdoors for the afternoon before an aide returns to put him into bed for the night. During their jaunt, the pair will roam acreage with wooded paths and rough tracks around fields where Rudy will park in tree shade and check electronic communications, perhaps chat with a neighbor, pray, while Maggie sniffs out another rabbit or deer to startle. So, overall, Rudy anticipates a satisfactory day, quite a good day, in fact—all things considered. •

Copyright 2022, Lois Elizabeth Hicks

Lois Elizabeth Hicks lives in rural Randolph County. Lois—a wife, mother, and grandmother—worked as a high school teacher and school media coordinator for many years while providing hands-on full care for an adult son paralyzed with quadriplegia. During those years she joined a 5-member Winston-Salem writing group and began journal entries of caregiving and respite day's events. She now writes nonfiction stories based on those journal events. Her story "What Happened to Judah Quinn?" appeared in the PSPP anthology, *Trouble*.

The Space Between
by David Inserra

How could this have happened? As I stood there, watching this woman I loved, my heart was breaking. My mother's wide blue eyes were filled with fear. She cupped her left hand and swept her right hand along the top of a clean counter, as if wiping cobwebs away.

"Look at this. How could they put me in this room?" She shook her empty cupped hand in my face. "This dust is everywhere." Her right hand pointed high, then low, as she crossed the hospital room and wiped her clean hands over the basket. "I don't understand what's happening."

She told me she woke last night to the sound of pounding. Men were making a coffin next to her bed. She pulled her covers over her head and waited for the darkness to fade. Later, my wife visited and took her for a walk. Stopping by a window in the hall, Mom pointed to the empty rooftop below. "Look at those children. How could their parents let them play on that roof?" She banged on the window. "The one with the striped shirt… He's too close to the edge!"

This all started rather simply. At the dinner table, with friends at the assisted living facility, Mom's speech became garbled. She fought for the right words but couldn't get her point across. The staff stepped in and called an ambulance.

After a few days in the hospital, her speech returned. We hoped things were going to improve. But they did not. Shortly thereafter, the hallucinations and paranoia stormed forth.

My brother and I met with the doctors who advised, for our mom's safety, she be moved to "Ward 6" where she could get the help she needed.

I got off the elevator, took a left, and approached a barricade, an imposing door with a small window, heavy twist handle, and a red light high over the frame.

When I picked up the phone on the wall, a calm voice asked, "Purpose?"

I gave my mom's name.

"Access."

After a soft click, the red light over the door turned green and I twisted the handle. These people believe that I am sane, so I am free to pass through the first set of doors and enter the space between, leaving the outside world behind. I closed the first door and waited. Another door confronted me, window to the left, heavy handle below it, red light above.

It's a simple, yet efficient, system. If a runner gets through this door, the short hall will be sealed, and the would-be escapee will be forced to return. I am not a runner. When the time comes to leave, the doors will open, and I will be set free. I smile to the security camera. Then I hear another click and another red light turns green.

As I enter this separated world, tension invades my chest. I feel helpless.

I can do nothing here. I have no skills. I have no power.

I see my mother's shrunken body shuffling through the crowd.

She passes a woman roaming about with lost, lifeless eyes, walking the hall with a silent visitor. Nearby is the "hello there" caller who greets everyone who passes. He sits with a small woman wearing a forced, tight-lipped smile. The "twig man" stands by his walker, carrying on an impassioned conversation, concern etched in his ancient face. No one is standing near him. No one listens to his words.

A blur of activity fills the hall. Some patients have visitors. Others are alone, existing only in a world of their own making.

I focus on my mom as she comes closer. I remember that sweet face before here. She grabs me with a hug, and we stand silent. Then we separate and find two chairs along a back wall. She tells me how sadness, fear, and anxiety are with her each day. She lived a caring, loving, and good life and can't understand why God has done this to her. She pleads with me for answers.

The Space Between

I have none to give.

Earlier, the therapist called and said Mom was making progress. Her brain was rewiring, coming back, he said. The hallucinations were fading, and she might soon be released to return to her life and her dog.

When I left, I stood in the space between the doors and watched my mother through the window as she melted back into the crowd of fellow patients. Were the hallucinations really gone? Did she know she was getting better? Could this all happen again? Would she join me at some point in this space in between? Would her smile at the security camera be returned with a soft click and a green light? Would the turning of the handle open the doors and set her free to join the world outside, beyond the imposing doors of "Ward 6"? •

Copyright 2022, David Inserra

David Inserra lives on Hilton Head Island in South Carolina. He enjoys his time with his wife, Ellen, and their dog, Mindy. He is a member of the Island Writers Network and works as the Congregational Administrator at the local Unitarian Church. Having recently completed his first novel, a speculative thriller titled "In Your Own Backyard," David is now editing the manuscript and working toward publication. David is also a musician who has written and recorded over 400 songs, most being about his wife. Visit davidinserra.weebly.com.

A Tap at My Door
by Rebecca S. Holder

"Help me?" The question was as soft and fearful and imploring as her beautiful brown eyes. In her hands were an empty pill bottle and a smartphone. Holding them forward, she repeated her plea. "Help me?"

Standing at my door was my new neighbor—a lovely young Middle Eastern woman, mother of 2- and 4-year-olds and wife to a much older naturalized citizen. Through broken English and a translation app, I learned her husband was in the Middle East on business for three months and she was almost out of medication. She and her children were alone in a country where they knew no one and she barely spoke the language.

I invited her in. A couple of phone calls and a very patient pharmacist later, I managed to get her prescription ordered and set-up on auto refill. Her relief was palpable as the fear and anxiety drained from her body. She sank down on the sofa. Thus began our three months of an immersive cultural exchange.

Food was carried back and forth almost daily—hers, richly aromatic traditional Arabic dishes, mine, down-home Southern fare sans pork. Her young boys had an instant affinity for my husband as he dropped to the floor among the toy cars, plastic dinosaurs, and building blocks to roughhouse and play while she looked on in amazement that a man would engage so freely with children. Through a video chat, we met her family across the ocean and a 7-hour time difference. We were honored guests at her son's third birthday party. We praised her first attempt at buttercream frosting.

Anissa's English improved exponentially, and our conversations grew longer and deeper, covering everything from hometowns and family to customs and lifestyles. Eventually we drifted into our respective beliefs and religions. Together we marveled at how much we had in common and how unimportant the differences seemed.

When the husband returned, he was surprised by her blossoming language skills and also suspicious of the friendships that had formed.

It has been a little over a year since her first tentative tap at my door. We have continued sharing and teaching our respective traditions—cooking the first Thanksgiving turkey, breaking the fast at Muharram with sweet rice, decorating a Christmas tree, and giving to charity at Ramadan. Even the everyday is a melding of cultures with my husband romping through the yard and digging worms with the boys as we sit on the patio sipping Arabic coffee flavored with cardamom.

The husband has come and gone—now gone for good. The divorce papers arrived from the Middle East via Federal Express. Instead of asking for my recipe for making lemon bars, she asked me how to set-up online accounts only she could access. Another neighbor guided her through paperwork at the children's school, the bank, an attorney, and for immigration.

Today she invited us to a most important event—her 5-year-old is graduating. She spoke about how proud and happy she is for this moment, what her plans are for the future, and why she is so grateful to my husband and me. It was only then I learned the magnitude of her courage in coming to my door, pleading for help. The husband had filled her with lies and self-doubt. We were white and would hate her because she is Muslim, he said. We could not be trusted, he assured her. We would harm her and her children, he warned. She was too stupid and weak-minded to learn English, he told her. She was incapable of anything and must do only what he said, he demanded. If she did not obey, she would suffer the consequences—he would break her, he threatened.

How great must have been her fear and desperation as she knocked on the door of someone she was told hated her and would hurt her? And how great was her courage and determination to push that thought aside, ignore a language barrier, and reach out into the unknown?

"Help me?" she asked. "Ok." I smiled. A brief moment—nothing dramatic, nothing extraordinary. Yet it was the

A Tap at My Door

moment when she made the decision not to return to her home country until she became an American citizen. It was the moment when she knew the rights and opportunities for her and her children would not be possible anywhere else. It was when confidence in herself and her abilities emerged, and the desire surfaced to stand strong. It was when taking control of her life and her future seemed possible.

It was also the moment when I recognized a remarkable truth, when I realized a single word or act of kindness can change the course of someone's life, when I understood we never know how these moments will come or appreciate where these moments might take us. My moment came as a tap at my door. I am glad I was there to answer. •

Copyright 2022, Rebecca S. Holder

Rebecca S. Holder lives in Winston-Salem, North Carolina, where she is a member of the Winston-Salem Writers. Early in her career, she wrote for corporate magazines, newspapers, and advertising agencies, but now writes for her own enjoyment. Currently she is writing a short story collection centered on the fictional town of Braidy Creek.

Editor's note:
"Anissa" is a pseudonym used to protect privacy.

Should I Go or Should I Stay?
by Emily Rosen

This is a recent experience I had in a doctor's office—and not for the first time.

Nurse, approaching quietly and whispering in my ear: "Mrs. Rosen, I think you made a mistake on your intake papers. You wrote Date-of-Birth as being 1927, and I think you might want to correct it."

Well, of course, I'd like to correct it. But, Lady. *It is what it is.*

Such was the initiation of my transitional thinking. Here I am, happily living alone, in the Sunshine State, in a totally Emily-functional 2-bedroom rental apartment no more than 15 "driving-during-the-day" minutes from everything I could ever need, including beaches, parks, birds, food emporia, and people. And I have a memory bank of travel and life experiences that could stuff several bookshelves of memoirs. (Those are yet to come.) I am especially grateful for volunteer activities to balance my lucky life, and the real bonus is relatively good health, an even temperament, and an absolute worship of mirth.

So, what's the problem? I refer you to paragraph two above—
so, no "mistakes." The *only* thing missing, is "family."
My remaining progeny lives in Charlotte, North Carolina, and
actuarial tables tease me with statistics. My friends—and I am
so fortunate to have many who are much younger than I—
assure me of their intention to "be there" for any emergency
needs I might require. Bless them.

Friends are great, but they all have their own lives, and I am an
integral part of the lives of my long-distance family. And with
the "*Big*" birthday pending, I made the wrenching decision
to pack it all up, and flee to Charlotte, this with the total
support, as well as hard to disguise, incredulity of "the family
of Florida friends." Not an inconsequential move, but one
entered with much thoughtfulness and consideration of the
strains of long-distance negotiations during end-of-life events.

I started the personal clean up, went so far as collecting
estimates from movers, made notes on what to take, what
to dispose of as largesse, what to sell, donate, and/or ditch,
and became somewhat paralyzed when I tried to organize my
bottomless collection of writings. I stopped long enough to
plan a trip to Charlotte to choose a new domicile, successfully
returning with an empowered determination to "do the deed."

And then, I woke up one morning just days after that visit, to
the TV punditry talking of the Ukrainian disaster. Immediately,
my 12-year-old-self popped into my vision on a September day
in 1939 when Grandma took me on a subway treat from
Brooklyn to visit a museum in the Bronx. As we exited the
building onto long descending concrete steps, we could hear

newspaper vendors hawking the news of the day in tones of urgency: "HITLER INVADES POLAND! Get your papers here. Read all about it."

"What's Poland, Grandma?" I asked. She sat me down on one of the myriad steps, rustled through the contents of her pocketbook and retrieved a picture of a little girl surrounded by a pastoral setting. She pointed to the picture with a sadness I'll never forget. "That's Poland," she said simply. Throughout the subsequent Holocaust years and beyond, that memory stings with the authenticity of fearsome beginnings. As it does now. And that was the moment my plans to move dissipated.

Much as I long to be with my family, the specter of an indefinite volatile economy suddenly struck me with panic. The uncertainty of all the social, economic, and emotional fallout from the daily horrors we are seeing in virtual real time have played havoc with my fantasy of a major lifestyle uprooting. The idea of dismantling my life while I am still in control of it lost its glamour. I decided to play "Russian Roulette," despite its unsavory appellation.

I feel the uneasy shaking of the walls of our planet as the apocalypse continues to rumble towards its unthinkable destination. I acknowledge the relative ant-like quality of my existence and continue to question the purpose of the genetic inclusion of evil, in greater and lesser degrees, into the DNA of the human species.

The senseless destruction, the stupid need for military buildup, the wasteful shelling out of enormous sums of money—so

Should I Go or Should I Stay

needed for other purposes—the inanity of the fact that such cataclysmic caution is considered to be normal for the preservation of nations is overwhelmingly grotesque to my simple ant-like mind.

Yes, I will "stay put" for now and work on getting my glass to its half-full status as it was back when I remembered that evil gets defeated in the l-o-n-g run. And if the "long-run" has a reasonably short shelf life, *Charlotte, here I come.* •

Copyright 2022, Emily Rosen

Emily Rosen lives in Boca Raton, Florida, where for over 20 years and until her recent 95th birthday, she instructed classes in memoir writing, publishing two anthologies of stories from her classes, and the book, *Who Am I?* For two decades and until the local weekly newspaper folded in 2021, she wrote the column "Everything's Coming Up Rosen." Her travel and feature articles have appeared nationwide while her poetry languishes in the pages of a fat notebook. She has worked as a copy writer, travel writer, columnist, elementary and community college teacher, mental health counselor, and owner of the now defunct "singing telegram" company, *Witty Ditty.* Her long-lived history puts her at an old Philco Radio listening to FDR's "Fireside Chats." (www.emilyrosen424.com)

The Thing About Life
by Alexandra Goodwin

"If I can make it there, I'll make it anywhere," sang Frank Sinatra of New York. Well, he wasn't born in Argentina. But I was.

Despite being an A+ student and a goody-two-shoes, higher education eluded me. I had dreams, and I wanted to be a writer. "You'll never be able to support yourself," my father said when I brought home the application for a Literature degree at the University of Buenos Aires.

We had a family meeting in which my sisters, mother, and father had opinions and a right to vote, a limited antidote to the dictatorship we were living under in 1980. Our democratic majority decided I should apply to the biology department instead and become a biologist. I excelled at science and had a knack for it. But when, incredulously, I failed my entrance exam, I was not surprised. *I get it.* Not everyone has a relative in high places with the master key to one's future.

Not one to give up, I enrolled in night classes to make sure I would pass the test next time. During the day, I worked as a bookkeeper in my father's stock brokerage firm. At the year's end, I walked into the exam room like I owned the place. A month later when I found out that the university had failed me again, I demanded, in person, to see my exam. Two armed police officers escorted me out and warned me never to come back. A second family meeting resulted in a unanimous decision that would drastically change the course of our family and my fate in particular. Within a year, we sold everything and moved to the United States.

Immigration laws in 1982 were tough and did not allow us four daughters to work on our student visas. Moreover, we were required to maintain full-time enrollment status even though credits cost us four times the rate American students paid. My father did some calculations, and this time, even though we were in America, he decided without a family meeting. He said our only chance was to pick a two-year-degree career, graduate, and then help with the living expenses. I became a legal secretary, got married, and buried my dreams.

Ten years ago, our son was pursuing a degree in Hospitality Management, when he dropped out of his freshman year and enrolled in Fire Academy instead. He became a firefighter, and, as is required by the State of Florida, he also became a paramedic. He applied to many jobs but never got one. Eventually, he was hired as a paramedic for a private ambulance company. That's when he fell in love with medicine. Whenever he had free time, he pulled out his medical books from under the driver's seat of the ambulance and swallowed them whole. A year later, he took a job as a paramedic in the emergency department of our city hospital, simultaneously pursuing a nursing degree so he could do more for the patients that came his way as a Registered Nurse. When doctors and nurses saw his passion in his work performance, many suggested he should become a doctor. But that seemed so farfetched, such an unreachable dream. We had used up his prepaid college tuition funds, he was no longer living at home, and his unconventional career path left him with degrees and certifications but no credits for pre-med required courses.

One afternoon I received a misdirected email—one never intended for me—saying that precisely that night would be the last in a week-long Medical Programs Fair at one of the convention centers in our county. We drove that night through relentless rain, and he connected with Bar Ilan University in Israel. He applied and was accepted to a one-year intensive pre-med program. A month later, our son had moved to Israel.

When he came back, he applied to medical school and graduated four years later. He had become a doctor.

During the recent pandemic, I contracted Covid. But my cough persisted even after I tested negative. My primary doctor dismissed it as "long Covid," but my son sent me for a specialized CT scan which revealed necrotic tissue behind my thyroid. A biopsy confirmed the dreaded diagnosis. I had surgery and will undergo further treatment. I will be okay.

The thing about life is this: when things happen, we have an opportunity to choose how we respond to both what we can change and what we cannot. In that way we write our life stories, each episode of disappointment and accomplishment a worthy entry into the whole.

As I recover from my surgery and treatments sitting under my mango tree, I am thankful for each obstacle and injustice that came my way.

Without them, I could not have written *this* story. •

Copyright 2022, Alexandra Goodwin

Alexandra Goodwin is a transplant from Buenos Aires, Argentina, and as such, nourishes her soul like an air plant without apparent roots. As she works toward semi-retirement, she has taken residence in her imaginary tree house above her mango tree in Florida. She's the author of *Exchange at the Border*, *Whispers of the Soul*, *What Color is Your Haiku?*, and *Caleidoscopio*. Her essays and poems have appeared or are upcoming in *Ariel Chart*, *The Centifictionist*, *Loch Raven Review*, *Stick Figure Poetry Quarterly*, *The Miami Herald* and others. www.alexandragoodwin.com

Dark Water
by Barbara Houston

The rented bus parked beside the North Wales Baptist Church in North Wales, Pennsylvania, where my dad was Pastor. The adult leaders loaded the picnic items onto the bus. The 13- to 16-year-olds swarmed around, anxiously waiting to get on the road for our day trip to the Pocono Mountains. Several small bags stuffed with bathing suits, towels, sunscreen, and bathing caps for the girls, were lying about on the sidewalk as the young people buzzed with excitement. Anticipating a day of adventure, the teens and chaperones boarded. The hour-and-a-half bus ride passed quickly as we sang songs, played jokes on one another, and laughed at the silly antics of some of the boys.

The area reserved for our outing was in a small alcove of the lake surrounded by beautiful, tall oak trees that shaded a wooden deck, picnic tables, changing rooms, and restrooms. Fifteen teens of assorted shapes and sizes raced to check out the lake sparkling in the sunlight. We then ran into the changing area, donned our bathing suits, and bounded toward the water. Excited shouts and giggles echoed throughout the woods and across the lake.

Although I could swim, I had always been cautious around lakes—the unknown lurking beneath the dark water held both fear and fascination for me. My friend, Maggie, who could not swim, and I stepped slowly into the water like young children taking our first tentative steps. We quickly forgot our fears as we splashed and laughed, totally unaware of hidden danger. The smell of hot dogs and hamburgers grilling over charcoal tickled our noses, inviting us to lunch. We ate voraciously, rested the required 30 minutes, and ran back into the lake.

Maggie led the way as we ventured farther away from shore.

"HELP! HELP!"

I looked up and saw Maggie frantically bobbing up and down, a dozen feet away. She had fallen into a "drop-off" and could not get out. I swam toward her, hopelessly fighting against the heavy weight of water. As I got close, she grabbed me, held on tenaciously, and pulled me under. We were both springing up and down like figures in a "jack-in-the-box."

I screamed for help, gulping in too much water each time I opened my mouth. Through a haze, I saw some of the other kids on the dock.

"Quit horsing around, you two!" someone yelled. Their laughter floated out across the water. I spotted one of the chaperones running toward the lake.

My body tensed as panic spread and terror seized me! Maggie held onto me, I flung my arms erratically, wildly reaching, searching for something, anything solid, to grab onto. My grasping hands found only cloudy water. It stung and burned my eyes and nostrils. My lungs felt as if they would burst as I choked and coughed, gasping for breath, relentlessly. Within seconds, the merciless lake swallowed me, then total darkness.

When I regained consciousness, I was lying on the dock. Greedily, I breathed in the cool mountain air. My friends surrounded me, their long faces revealing deep concern. Through blurry vision, I focused on Maggie who was standing over me panting for breath. Tears rolled down her cheeks. Somehow, she had outwitted the perilous water and pulled us both out of the hole to safety. The chaperone had carried me to shore and resuscitated me. Maggie and I cried and hugged, thinking about what could have happened.

Emotionally exhausted, I was silent on the ride back. My near-death experience played over in my mind like a movie. I just wanted to be home, to cry on my mother's shoulder, and to feel her loving arms wrapped around me, assuring me that I was safe.

The nightmares began immediately. In the dreams I relived the terror, and just as I blacked out, I would wake up screaming. My mother would run to my bed and comfort me. Eventually the nightmares stopped.

Since that day, I no longer swim in lakes or oceans. I choose the safety of a swimming pool where I can swim to the edge and grab onto something solid. I panic if someone dunks me. When I hear stories of people drowning, I remember my

Dark Water

feelings. I visualize the helplessness and fear of their last moments.

I do not know if the events of that day affected Maggie the way they did me. We lost touch after my family moved. But I am grateful that my friend, Maggie, saved both of us that day. Although the dark lake tried to claim us, fate had other plans. The girl who could not swim saved the one who could. The dark water lost its two intended victims. •

Copyright 2022, Barbara Houston

Barbara Houston lives in Charlotte, North Carolina. A member of Scribblers, a memoir writing group, she writes stories about her life. In her varied career she taught school, coordinated volunteers for non-profits, conducted training classes for non-profits, and served as a Director of Human Resources. Now retired, she enjoys writing, reading fiction, singing with The Charlotte Singers, spending time with family and friends, and traveling with her husband, Jerry. Barbara's first two published stories "In Bear Country" and "Music Box Memories" appeared in the PSPP anthologies *Trouble* and *Curious Stuff*.

Morgan: Our Escape Artist
by Janet K. Baxter

My love of animals runs deep in my soul. This passion triggered a decision that propelled our family into an escapade spanning 16 years.

While at the veterinarian's office with my son's dog, I glanced over the bulletin board with its numerous hand-written notices and business cards. A note captured my attention: "Free dog, Golden Retriever, 1-year-old male, neutered." I wanted a dog to accompany me on runs, so the next day I called the number listed and made an appointment to see the dog.

The owner led me to his back yard. Morgan was a beautiful golden-mix, long-haired with a thick undercoat that needed a good brushing. He was friendly, well-fed, and exuberant. Morgan was in a small, fenced back yard, but was also chained to a tree. The owner told me Morgan kept leaping the fence and that he had to keep the dog chained or Morgan would be off down the street. He felt bad that the dog was chained and wanted a better situation for him. Of course, I promptly put Morgan in my car and took him home.

We put Morgan in the small kennel in our back yard, fed him, and left him to settle in. Within minutes, the children ran into the house shrieking that Morgan had leaped over the kennel and was running around the house. We had an "escape artist" on our hands! Clearly, other accommodations were needed.

Over that summer, my husband, Michael, built a tall, stout, wooden fence around the back yard. A wooden gate between the back yard and the driveway kept Morgan safely inside the fence. Or so we thought!

Morgan climbed over the fence.

Michael added a one-foot extension on the top of the fence.

Morgan dug under the fence.

Michael attached chicken-wire to the fence and dug a foot into the ground to prevent Morgan from digging out.

Morgan chewed through the gate.

After each addition, my husband proudly proclaimed that, *this time,* Morgan would not get out. Every time Morgan escaped, we found this adolescent pup lying on the front porch looking quite pleased with himself. During that school year, Morgan often greeted our children at the school bus stop which was two blocks from our home. He escorted them home and the kids would put him back in the back yard. They took great glee in taunting their dad, "Morgan got out, again!"

At last, Michael built fencing secure enough to contain Morgan. But Morgan was not happy. He missed his escapades and wanderings around the neighborhood. When I reached for his leash, Morgan would jump about, wildly excited, his tail wagging furiously. He did enjoy running with me, although it took a bit of training to get his bounding and youthful enthusiasm restrained enough that he wasn't towing me around the subdivision like a weaving trailer fishtailing behind a speeding truck.

Morgan was with us as each of our children matured and left home. He shared in our adjustment to our much quieter house. However, it wasn't until later that by accident we found a solution to Morgan's unhappiness. We found good property to keep my horses, something near local horse trails. We purchased seven acres with an existing house that needed much upgrading. We built a small barn for the horses and installed invisible fencing to keep the dogs within the acre surrounding the house and barn. Morgan and my new young trail dog, Meara, quickly adapted to their new home and learned to stay within its boundaries.

That was when we began noticing a change in Morgan. Multiple times a day, our aging mate walked the perimeter of the invisible fence line checking for errant, potential predators. In the evenings and throughout the night, Morgan patrolled inside the house, going from room to room checking on us. He would sleep near us at night unless the grand-girls were visiting. Then he abandoned us, and we'd find him guarding the girls. It was then we realized that, although Morgan was probably a mix of Golden Retriever and Collie, he was also part working guardian dog. His personal job, as he took it, was to check out and guard the property—and his family. Within the invisible fencing system, he was able to look out over the boundary and check the borders. He could finally do his job without that pesky wooden fence getting in the way!

Morgan did all of his jobs well and lived on our "mini-estate" for many years. Michael's hard work was worth it as Morgan accompanied him on walks, supervised his gardening while under the shade of a tree, lay at his feet while reading in the back yard, and did sentry duty during our raucous family gatherings. He was, as we always told him, "a good boy."

After 16 years, Morgan made his "final escape."
We miss him always. •

Copyright 2022, Janet K. Baxter

Janet K. Baxter lives in Kings Mountain, North Carolina, and is a member of the Charlotte Writer's Club and Scribblers, a memoir critique group. Her stories, "Horse Whispering for the Average Woman," "Southern Blues," "A Frank Lesson," "Cappie, The Boomerang Horse," and "An Angel's Smile" have appeared in previous anthologies published by the Personal Story Publishing Project. Retired, Janet enjoys her new passion, thread painting, as well as dabbling in writing, trail riding, and keeping up with all the critters on her "mini-estate:" www.mountaingaitacres.com.

Putting Everything on the Line
by Deirdre Garr Johns

The letter arrived by certified mail, its delivery assured and unquestionable. And even though I had waited many months for this letter, I was reluctant to open it. I was not ready to decide.

I hoped for a "no." It would be simpler—nothing to choose. It was a "yes" I feared.

Opening the letter, I learned I was indeed accepted into pharmacy school. All I needed to do was sign and return. But I hesitated. Recent experiences in two courses created a conflict I was not expecting.

I was out of my element with no labs, no goggles, no chemicals. This room had no windows, and the carpet was a dirty, dark green. I felt uncomfortable. Dr. Sorentin entered the classroom, leaned against a desk, and stared at us. She gave her speech, a memorized one perfected over many semesters.

"I know about the posters plastered throughout the dorms," she said. "They advise you not to take my writing class. There will be daily assignments that require reading and writing and

time. If you aren't going to do the work, leave now."
She waved her arm toward the door.

I admired her demanding confidence, her commanding presence. But I was hoping for an easy class, one that would complete my application to pharmacy school. Leaving was not an option with just two semesters left.

Later that morning, my Organic Chemistry professor, Dr. Roberts, also began class with a speech: "Look to your left. Look to your right. By the end, only one of you will remain. The closer you sit to the genius—a.k.a. me!—the better you will perform."

His analysis for our success was bleak, but the next class meeting demonstrated our assessment of his hypothesis: the first few rows of the auditorium were full. We were pulled front-and-center as if our lives depended on it.

As I held the acceptance letter, I should have felt joy. Everything I planned for my future was mine—if I signed. That blank signature line represented everything—an end and a beginning. Putting my name on it would start a new life. But I was already experiencing a new beginning. Something else—something unexpected—had taken me over when I found myself a student in Dr. Sorentin's writing class.

Without my signature, I had two possible futures. Signing meant I was committing to one. How could I determine such a thing at 20 years of age?

I set the letter aside and understood joy and heartache beating together as one.

Letting go of a long-held dream is not easy, but I was no longer convinced that my place in this world was in the lab. And I was too afraid to acknowledge the possibility of an alternative, which nagged at me each time I walked into Dr. Sorentin's class. Despite her harsh, initial approach, she had begun to mentor me and to nurture my writing in just a few short weeks. Even after many months in the science building, I could not say I had found the same there.

This nagging—the possibility of becoming an English major— was not practical. It created an uncertain future. What would I do with an English degree? Surely not be a teacher.

After all, my high school guidance counselor told me with certainty that English majors became teachers. Perhaps I thought it would be too limiting. So, I closed that door and set my sights on a field that would eliminate the possibility.

But I could not ignore the fact that Dr. Sorentin saw something in me—in my writing—that was worth noting. Her response to my writing was a catalyst (something I learned about in science). I realized that while I was good at writing lab reports, science and I did not have much chemistry. We didn't bubble, change color, or explode when we mixed. Maybe I just needed a clearer vision and the confidence to walk through another door that was opening to me.

It was no coincidence that both my writing and Organic Chemistry classes occurred in the same semester. This was exactly what I needed to see what was really on the line—my happiness. And while I was unsure about what I would do with an English degree, for the first time I was excited to choose my classes. I did not see them as boxes to check off like I did when scheduling classes for pharmacy school.

Taking the uncertain path led me with confidence to where I belong—in the classroom. Each year, I rejoice in greeting my students as they walk through my door. I want to see something in them just as Dr. Sorentin saw in me. And I hope to inspire them to keep all doors open and to be willing to put everything on the line for the sake of their happiness. •

Copyright 2022, Deirdre Garr Johns

Deirdre Garr Johns resides in Hilton Head, South Carolina with her husband and son. She is a teacher by trade, and she began writing more seriously in recent years. Nature is a source of inspiration, and her work often includes memories of people and places. Her poetry and non-fiction have appeared in several magazines and anthologies, and she is currently working on her first poetry collection.
Her website is amuseofonesown.com, which includes published works and personal reflections, including "The 6-word story: trial and error"—a playful story about names.

The Saltwater Taffy Escapade
by Patricia E. Watts

When I was in 6th grade, my older brother, Arnie, saw an article in our local Colorado newspaper about the YMCA offering a chance to earn a free week at camp by selling saltwater taffy. Saying he was "pumped" about trying this adventure would be an understatement. And, being a good sister, I decided I would go with him. We walked untold miles and knocked on too many doors. No territory in town was off limits, so we covered eastside, northside, then the southside. All told, Arnie had sold the most saltwater taffy in the history of our city. He earned not one, but *three* weeks of camp. He also got a beautiful green jacket and his picture on the Wall of Honor at the YMCA. And being a good brother, Arnie gave me one of his three weeks.

His two weeks of camp in the beautiful Rocky Mountains came first. Not only did he have a wonderful camp experience, but he came home with the coveted Archery award. My week came next and after hearing Arnie's stories I was ready to make my own glorious camp adventures. I arrived and settled in for orientation. I met new campers and picked out my bunk in one of the rustic cabins. We learned the camp rules, what our dining room chores would be, and what our schedule of activities would be for the week. Our days would start each morning with a shower before breakfast.

That shower was an enclosed rudimentary shower only a short trek from the cabin. The fresh mountain water dispensed was ice cold. If it's possible, I think my goosebumps had their own goosebumps. It was that miserable. I wasn't looking forward to that every morning. But I gritted my teeth and thought, *I can do this. One shower down, six to go.*

We spent the first day getting to know one another, making crafts, and playing fun games. We all looked forward to the horseback trip through the mountains the next day. Next morning, we were assigned our mounts to ride, and our camp guide gave us riding instructions. I could do this. After all, I had watched many hours of black-and-white cowboy movies on television. Halfway up the mountainside we crossed a stream. My horse lost his footing and fell in the creek, dumping me in the water as well. As he scrambled to right himself, "the brute" stepped on my foot giving me an excruciating, painful injury. I'd never seen a horse fall in a creek in the movies unless the cowboy was shot. I thought, *Well, at least I don't have to walk back to camp. And I didn't get shot.* Not much comfort, though.

The next day was the much-anticipated Archery competition. I had dreams of bringing home a prize to put beside my older brother's prize. At least I could hobble on my sore foot and still compete. Try as I might, I could not shoot the arrow far enough to reach the target let alone get a bullseye. What a disappointment. No glorious recognition for me.

Back at camp, our cabins did not have screens on the windows, just big, wooden shutters to close when it rained or to throw open at night for welcoming the wonderful night air with no pests. Although I was having trouble falling asleep that night because of my painful foot, eventually the gentle night breeze soothed me into a deep sleep. What I did not know was that the horses were turned out to pasture each night. So, when a wandering horse stuck his head in through my open window and snorted right in my face, I let out a scream heard across the whole camp. I did not know I could jump out of bed so fast, sore foot or not. After everyone settled back down, I thought, *Well, at least it was just a horse. Could have been a bear.* Not much comfort in that either.

Our last outing was a day-long hike to a beautiful waterfall. We finished breakfast, packed our lunches, and set off. My foot still hurt and by the time we got back to camp I was in worse shape than when I had started, only to discover I now had a bad case of athlete's foot from that shower. More than ever, I was ready to go home.

That "free" week of camp was expensive. It cost me many hours of knocking on doors, and provided a miserable week of cold showers, two horse scares, a wounded foot, and no archery award to match my brother's. I think I actually paid for my free week in more ways than I knew. I thought, *I should stick to watching black-and-white cowboy movies and just eat the saltwater taffy myself.*

That would be some comfort. •

The Saltwater Taffy Escapade

Copyright 2022, Patricia E. Watts

Patricia E. Watts lives in Mountville, South Carolina where the love of local and family history has given her a passion to write stories to pass down to her children. She has found through stories of tragedies, tears, and triumphs and even mysteries that she has a rich heritage worth telling. Five stories have appeared in previous PSPP anthologies: "A Real Small Town," the paired stories "Sometimes the Prize Goes to the Wrong Person" and "The Orphan Train," "Chancing the Buddy System," and "The Class of '44 Ring."

Right Turn at a Funeral
by M.J. Norwood

As I sat on the front row pew between my husband and my two fidgeting children, I started praying. *Oh Lord, please don't let me cry.* In front of me, was a modest gray casket, topped with a lovely spray of white Chrysanthemums and Baby's Breath. It contained the remains of my 81-year-old father-in-law, a veteran of World War II as well as the teaching profession. Beloved by his students and colleagues, he taught elementary school and served as a principal for 40 years.

Our church pastor was speaking, but I wasn't listening. I had to be strong. I forced my mind to wander. I thought about my mother-in-law, who had passed away only a few months before. That was sad, too. I thought about my having quit my job to look after my father-in-law. He had dementia. I selfishly thought about the fact that I would now have to find a new job.

The wandering-mind strategy was not working very well in helping control my emotions. *My poor children.* They had grown used to Granddaddy being in the house. *My poor husband. My poor sister-in-law.* Poor me. How sad.

I diverted my attention further, thinking of other things.
I grew up visiting practically every museum in the state and knew that is where I would one day work. I knew from the beginning of college that I would major in history, wear funny clothes and talk to people about old stuff. And that's what I did. I was interviewed at Colonial Williamsburg the day after I graduated. I was a historical interpreter that summer, then took a job at Old Salem, back home in North Carolina. I spent 20 years dyeing yarn and making baskets, happily content to do that for the rest of my life. I married the blacksmith at Old Salem. He wore funny clothes, too. We bought a house in the country and had two children. Life was perfect, until my father-in-law started forgetting things. When his wife passed away, we knew he could not live alone.

W*ait. A silent pause. What was going on? The next speaker.* Oh, yes, the kind Moravian minister we had met at the hospital, after my father-in-law suffered a stroke. After seeing the name of his favorite elementary school teacher on the hospital list, he had made a beeline for the low-lit room where our family sat in silence. His warm and caring smile brightened our spirits. "Mr. Norwood? Not my former teacher, it can't be," he said.

He explained that Wilson Norwood had not only changed his life but had saved his life. "He turned me around," he said. He declared he owed everything to Mr. Norwood. He seemed so genuinely grateful that after my father-in-law's peaceful passing my sister-in-law asked if he would like to say a few words at the funeral.

That minister towered above a filled church as he stepped into place. He said nothing for what seemed an eternity as those assembled quieted themselves.

I was unprepared for the eulogy that followed. Instead of a few kindly remembrances, this wise man presented a heartfelt tribute to the pedagogical profession. He explained that a teacher was more than someone who drilled information into you to be regurgitated on a test. A teacher was more than a disciplinarian. He reminded us that we each remembered one special teacher, one who did something that showed they genuinely cared. For this speaker, that teacher was my father-in-law.

He said Wilson Norwood was the kind of educator whose compassion went beyond the classroom. He got to know his students and their families by visiting them in their homes. He taught students to care, not only for others, but for themselves, by showing them that he cared. He taught them the most important asset in life. He taught them how to learn.

When the speaker concluded his remarks, knowing sighs and murmurs of agreement filled the sanctuary along with love—love not only for a special teacher but for all special teachers, and for the teaching profession. I knew, right then, what I had to do.

Six weeks later, I was hired as a teacher assistant. I never asked about the salary in the interview. I didn't care. I knew at age 42 I wanted to be the kind of teacher who made a difference.

Right Turn at a Funeral

I went back to school and earned a master's degree in library science. I became a teaching librarian. That allowed me to reach every student. I knew I could never be the teacher Wilson Norwood had been, but the standard he set was one for which I would strive.

And just like Wilson Norwood had done for him, that Moravian minister, speaking in a Baptist church, changed the direction of my life. I can only pray that I might do the same for at least one of my students. •

Copyright 2022, M.J. Norwood

Recently retired after 14 years of service to the students at East Bend Elementary School, M.J. Norwood lives in East Bend, North Carolina. Her work has appeared in the Personal Story Publishing Project publication, *Curious Stuff*, and she is the author of *The Sandbar* and *The Shoals*. A member of the North Carolina Writers' Network and currently writing her third book, she loves nothing more than being recognized and remembered by former students.

Kitty Gets a Name
by Joel R. Stegall

I was deep into a household project for which I was woefully under-qualified. Once my wife said it would be nice for our fireplace's slate hearth to be repaired, I took it as a challenge to do it myself, undeterred by my utter lack of experience.

With the confidence of the ignorant, I decided I would need a small bag of mortar mix and that I needed it right then, no matter that we were in a thunderstorm about as heavy as it ever gets in Winston-Salem. What should have been a routine trip to Home Depot became a life-altering experience.

Barely able to see in the downpour as I stopped at a major intersection, I waited for the light to change so I could turn left. Right between two traffic lanes, among bits of debris, I noticed an unusual black clump. As I looked more closely, I saw that it was a shivering kitten curled up into a drenched, wet furball. I was sure that in the next few seconds this pitiful baby was going to be squashed.

Miraculously, when the light changed, the kitten was still there. As I moved forward in the left turn lane, I stopped beside the terrified animal, opened the door, reached down, scooped it up, and put it by my feet. This all took maybe three seconds, but the driver behind me, oblivious to what was going on, leaned on his horn, irritated that I was disrupting the flow of traffic. As I took my left turn and continued toward Home Depot, the kitten, maybe four weeks old, sat immobile, making not a sound. Then it let out a little poop. I was hooked. Anything that poops in my car has my attention.

The immediate danger was over, but what to do now? For a moment, I thought of taking the distressed creature home with me. Then I remembered that kittens need to be fed. They need a place to sleep. And there would be kitty poop on the carpet. And vet bills. Even more to the point, neither my wife nor I had ever lived with animals in the house, and we had no real desire to start now. Then I got choked up, thinking of this helpless baby, lost and without its mother. For the second time in one day, I had gotten myself involved with something outside my experience, and way above my pay grade.

The animal shelter takes in homeless animals, right? Maybe the kitten could find a new home there. On the other hand, I had no idea where the animal shelter was. Further, I had recently read that something like 90% of the animals that go to a shelter are put to sleep after a week. The shivering, furry, lovable thing at my feet deserved better, but I had no idea what that might be.

As the downpour continued, I went on to Home Depot, where I left the kitten in the car and went inside to find the mortar mix. As I walked by the customer service desk, some force urged me to talk to the folks there. I told them my story and asked if anyone knew where the animal shelter was. One woman seemed more than casually interested. She wanted to know the kitten's color. When I told her it was black, she said her black, male cat had recently died of cancer and she was looking for a new pet. By this time, the rain had subsided a bit and she went to the car with me to look at the kitty for whose life I was now responsible. This woman I had known for no more than five minutes fell in love with the kitten. Her eyes filled with tears of joy as she picked up this small, wet, scared, beautiful, black ball of fur and held it closely in her arms. I had to hold back my own tears. Through all this, the kitten never let out a whimper.

Back inside Home Depot, as the woman dried off her new baby, she discovered it was a boy. As I was about to say goodbye, she asked my name. When I told her, she said her new kitten would also be "Joel."

A friend told me later that this was a sign of God's work. I am a bit uncomfortable with that language, thinking that God must have more important things to attend to than lost kittens. But I wonder. I often get involved with things I don't understand, like home repair projects. And sometimes someone, or some thing, such as a cold wet kitten, intrudes to offer a totally unexpected chance to do a good thing.

And, yes, the fireplace did get repaired. •

Copyright 2022, Joel R. Stegall

Joel R. Stegall's start in graduate school was cut short by an invitation from the U.S. Army to help save the world from Communism after the Berlin Wall went up in 1961. After serving two years as a lieutenant, he taught music in junior high school, which he discovered was much more difficult than commanding troops. Moving into higher education, Joel held teaching and administrative posts in North Carolina, New York, Florida, and Virginia. Since retiring to Winston-Salem, North Carolina, he sings in two choirs and writes on occasion.

A Divine Dating Detour
by Sarah H. Clarke

I had given up. Life was good after all, even if solo. It was time to stop dredging Charlotte's online dating pool of single-for-a-reason, 40-ish-year-old men. I deleted my accounts. As a teleworker, online student, and introverted homebody, if I were to meet my life partner, the Universe would just have to be creative.

It was months later that I stumbled upon a podcast interview with anthropologist, Dr. Helen Fisher. She had studied couples behavior for over 30 years and consulted on the creation of a dating site, *Chemistry.com*. It recommended matches based on "human chemistry," determined by the results of a personality test. Fascinated, I immediately looked up the site and registered, not with the intention of meeting someone, but to take the test. As a psychology buff and eternal self-discoverer, I took every personality test I came across. It was a compulsion.

Before I could finish reading my test results, match notifications began coming in. I ignored them initially, but curiosity eventually bested me. There was something about one guy, in particular. His picture showed him looking soulfully off into the distance, radiating a gentle nature with a handsome side view and ruddy cheeks. I found him so captivating that I uploaded photos of myself, completed my profile, and messaged the intriguing stranger.

The next morning, my email was full of match messages from a different dating site called *OkCupid*. I was confused but assumed my email address had been shared between sites. I had to create an account to get in and see what was going on. It seemed legit and was free, so I uploaded pictures and completed my profile on that site too. *Fine, why not?*

A spring beach trip with girlfriends was a welcome distraction from my oft obsessive mind. I had received no response from the intriguing stranger.

I did, however, receive a long, letter-like message from a guy on *OkCupid*. It began with, "I am a well-educated, highly intelligent professor…" *Interesting.* "I also rescue kittens, puppies, and baby bunnies from burning buildings in my spare time." *Witty.* The letter writer went on to describe himself, contend that we seemed to have a lot in common and might have fun talking over a glass of wine. I had already seen him on the site, however, and wasn't interested. It was his pictures: two in a series of emphatic, toothy selfies oriented sideways because, his captions said, he couldn't figure out how to straighten them. *He's highly intelligent and can't figure out how to rotate a photo?* I was positive he was not my type. Besides, experience had taught me that long, expressive messages were usually meant to compensate for some hideously undesirable trait that would be exposed on the first date—like squishy, bizarre mannerisms or bad teeth. I delayed addressing his message, still hoping the intriguing stranger would respond.

After some time, I did respond and accept the professor's invitation, for no other reason than appreciation for an eloquently written letter. *We probably would have fun talking—once.* The date was set for the night after my return from the beach.

Tired and sunburned, the dreaded commitment loomed over me. *I could be curled up on my couch right now*, I lamented, driving around looking for some elusive wine bar.

Stepping into the venue, I took in the small, ambient space. Front and center, a man stood up. A man with a broad chest in a blue plaid shirt. My eyes lifted to meet the most tender, soulful gaze of the softest blue. I recognized him, I thought—like someone I loved deeply long ago, in a hazy, *de-ja-vu* sense. We smiled, introduced ourselves, and settled beside each other on a leather couch. He was as articulate and warm as he was handsome, with a feature I did not notice immediately in the warm, low-lit room—ruddy cheeks.

Like long-lost friends, we excitedly shared what we had been up to all those years apart. He had five children. I had two. He was a lawyer and professor, preparing for a trip to Lithuania as a visiting scholar. I was an IT business consultant, studying Applied Anthropology, and preparing for a volunteer trip to Thailand to work with captive elephants. Hours fell away. Only as the bar announced closing did we remember where we were.

A Divine Dating Detour

The next several years shot rapid fire, life-altering trials at each of us, which we overcame through the steadfast support of one another. When our lives finally settled down, we married, coincidentally, five years to the day of our first date.

Yes, the professor was, in fact, the "intriguing stranger." Having abandoned his *Chemistry.com* profile, he never received my message. Even so, he had been reaching out for me, too.

Reflecting on the string of events that brought us together, I can't help but smile. The Universe had most certainly been creative. •

Copyright 2022, Sarah H. Clarke

Sarah H. Clarke lives in Charlotte, North Carolina and is a member of the Charlotte Writers Club. She blogs on the subject of Complex Post Traumatic Stress Syndrome (CPTSD) at www.sarahhclarke.com as well as for the CPTSD Foundation. Sarah and her husband have seven children between them and live in an 18th century home that they all restored together. International travel, continuous learning, creativity, and being in nature are among her passions. Sarah has two stories published through the Personal Story Publishing Project.

One Day's Notice
by Ken Chamlee

Most couples expecting a child enjoy a few months of eager anticipation and planning. They ready a colorful nursery, friends throw them a baby shower, and grandparents-to-be make helpful suggestions for names. Even weeks out, the due date is a good marker for the life-changing event.

My wife and I had one day. One day from no prep and no nursery to "Welcome Home, Baby." Zero-to-sixty parenthood. That is the way adoption sometimes works.

That glorious, hectic day, though sudden, was six years in the making. When my wife and I first learned that we would never be able to conceive, we were devastated. Many hard days and decisions followed, but eventually we chose our path. We attended an adoption information meeting of the Children's Home Society of North Carolina, the state's leading agency. The news was bleak. Very few babies were available.

"Come back in two years," they said.

We went on with our lives, many of our friends had babies,

and we waited. After 24 months we drove to Asheville for another CHS adoption meeting. "Come back in two years," they said again. It is a humbling experience to know that something so normal and common as having a child will be denied you, and that even raising a child might not be possible. So many babies planned and wanted; so many unplanned and perhaps unwanted. But none to be yours.

Another two years passed, we returned for a third information session. None of the couples we had seen before was there. "All right," the representatives said. "We will talk to you. No promises." What followed were months of interviews, writing our personal histories, our friends and families being interviewed, statements of stability requested from our employers. What some people do so easily, or even accidentally, we were tested and judged for worthiness. But we understood; children are the most precious resource, and the agency had every reason to be scrupulous.

At long last, we received the letter we had hoped for all those years. "We will place a child with you," it read, "sometime in the next 18 months." Joy! But more waiting. "We will call you," the letter also said, "and you will come to Greensboro the next day."

Whoa. Instant parenthood. One day's notice. Imagine being indefinitely pregnant. No due date. Just the knowledge of a delivery at some point. We had a choice: get everything ready for our baby now and look at the toys and the clothes and the crib every day, or not subject ourselves to a happy but relentless anticipation. We chose the latter.

The next October, I was camping in Cades Cove with a faculty colleague during our fall break. We rose early to shoot photographs of deer browsing in the meadow-mist. It was cool, quiet, peaceful. When we arrived back in Brevard late Sunday afternoon, two fellow English teachers were waiting at my friend's house. That's odd, I thought, especially when they started unloading his gear from my truck with a great deal more celerity than care.

"You need to go home," they said. "NOW." For a second, I had that pit-of-the-stomach feeling that some tragedy had happened, but they were smiling and ignoring my friend's pleas to be careful with his camera equipment. I raced across town. My wife was standing in the driveway with her purse and two suitcases.

"We have a son," she said through happy tears. "We have to go to Greensboro right now. I packed for you." The call had come the day before. Every single friend we had knew I was a father before I did. She had even called the National Park Service in the Great Smokies to locate me but by the time they figured out where I was, my buddy and I had already broken camp.

"I need a shower," is all I could say, overcome. A blur of a drive, a near-sleepless night (merely the first), and the next day we were parents, trying to fit our 10-week-old baby into the newborn onesie we had brought. Andrew Paul's lungs proved in fine working order. That night we were back in Brevard, and Andrew slept his first few nights in an emptied dresser drawer padded with towels and blankets. Our "labor" had lasted over six years, years scattered with disappointment and heartbreak,

One Day's Notice

but finally elation. We were well aware, too, that somewhere in the state a young mother we would never meet had made the brave choice to place her child for adoption, and four lives were forever changed.

We raised our son with all the love and struggle two people might expect. But we always had a good story to tell about that flip-the-switch day and the thrilling shock of instant parenthood. •

Copyright 2022, Kenneth Chamlee

Kenneth Chamlee's work has appeared in three previous Personal Story Publishing Project collections, and his poems have been in *North Carolina Literary Review, Tar River Poetry, Cold Mountain Review, Pinesong, Kakalak*, and in many other places. He is a 2022 Gilbert-Chappell Distinguished Poet for the North Carolina Poetry Society and teaches regularly for the Great Smokies Writing Program of UNC-Asheville. A book of poems, *If Not These Things*, is forthcoming from Kelsay Books in 2022. Learn more at www.kennethchamlee.com and @kenchamlee on Twitter.

Losing Sight
by Marci Spencer

"**Y**ou can't see what?" I asked.

"I can't see the instruments," my husband said, setting up his final approach to land our Cessna-172 Skyhawk at Shiflet Field, a small grass airstrip outside Marion, North Carolina.

As a diversionary escape from our medical careers—he, an orthopedic surgeon, and I, a nurse practitioner—we often took a pleasure flight on Sunday afternoons. We both had earned our private pilot licenses, but his Type-A personality always seemed to take the lead position and fly as the pilot-in-command. *A man thing, I believe.*

I knew his advanced IFR training had prepared him to pilot an aircraft solely by reading the instruments—a critical asset in poor weather. My basic VFR training only allowed me to pilot a plane on clear days, using visual references, such as topographical cues and landmarks. But, on that cloudless September day with fall colors exploding across the Western North Carolina hillsides, the visibility appeared endless. Clear skies. Light and variable winds. I could have piloted the plane that day, but my easy-going personality quietly acquiesced and slipped into the cockpit as the navigator.

After a peaceful cruise, John headed back to Shiflet Field. After paralleling the airstrip on the downwind position, he began to bank into the base leg when his vision failed. The instrument panel became blurry. With the plane configured for landing and our turn onto final approach imminent, we remained mentally focused to handle the sudden change in our situation. With his steady hands on the control wheel, I announced the airspeed, altitude, and other instrument readings as we brought the plane into a soft landing and roll out. We were down—safely.

John's loss of vision signaled a worrisome, altered course in our self-programmed compass heading of hopes and dreams. Within the month, John had a massive stroke, leaving him with partial paralysis, blindness, confusion, and garbled speech. *Had we not seen the signs coming or did we just ignore them?* For decades, we had diagnosed disorders and managed patient care for others. Now, at 54-years-old, we were the patient and caregiver. *How do we find ourselves again? Who are we? What is our life's purpose?*

Down deep, his Type-A lifestyle channeled his competitive, self-motivated instincts into the physical therapy and speech therapy sessions, regaining some functions. But the permanent loss of visual acuity and mental alertness prevented him from driving a car or managing domestic functions. While providing him the supportive care that he needed to attain the best quality of life, I needed to abandon my passive nature and become our pilot-in-command on our new course in life. I became his outspoken patient care advocate, addressing his health care needs involving multiple medical specialists.

At the same time, I searched for my own space, an outlet that embraced my deepest core and personal identity. I found that space, that peace, among the red spruce and Fraser fir trees on top of the highest mountain in Great Smoky Mountains National Park. One day a week, I immersed myself in the outdoor world, volunteering as a national park volunteer. There, I introduced visitors from around the world to the natural history of pine siskins, red crossbills, black bears, balsam woolly adelgids, Carolina northern flying squirrels, and red-cheeked salamanders. Tourists from 5 to 85 posed myriad questions. I made notes and stuck them in my uniform pockets if I did not have the answer, so I could research the material back home. My notebooks filled with the cultural history and natural history of Clingmans Dome became my first published book. I had found my voice, a place to be me. I began writing one book after another on the history of our national forests.

John and I have reversed our prior roles and life responsibilities. We don't fly airplanes anymore. On the fields here at the farm, where we had planned to build a hanger and an airstrip after we retired, we raise livestock and bale hay. Medical complications keep life interesting, of course. So does John's stubborn, independent machismo, surfacing from time to time. Once, after John's paralyzed foot slipped off the tractor's brake pedal, sending him into the farm pond, he rigged the tractor's mechanics to operate only on the left side. Another time, John grabbed a rat snake with his one capable hand to toss it out of the barn. In an instant, the serpent rascal wrapped itself around John's arm, trying to subdue its predator. It turned its gaping mouth toward John's thumb and bit it. The tough, one-handed farmer bit it back to make it loosen its grip on him.

We lost sight of our future in the plane that day, but we have tapped into our inner resources to navigate our new life's journey together.

Still, I suggest not biting a snake. The taste is awful, I'm told. In my books about our national forests, I promote a more civil approach to our wild friends. •

Copyright 2022, Marci Spencer

A native of Asheville, North Carolina, now living in Old Fort, Marci Spencer grew up on land that her great-grandfather refused to sell to George Vanderbilt for the Biltmore Estate. She worked as a nurse practitioner in the fields of cardiology, family medicine, and overseas medical missionary service. After hiking hundreds of miles, volunteering for the park service, and earning certification as a naturalist/environmental educator, Marci wrote *Clingmans Dome, Highest Mountain in the Great Smokies*, *Pisgah National Forest: a History*, *Nantahala National Forest: a History*, and *Pisgah Inn*—all published by Arcadia Publishing/History Press.

Finding Home
by Karen Luke Jackson

The first time I stepped into the "Sanctuary in the Pines," a retreat center at Highland Lake Cove in Flat Rock, North Carolina, the place felt like home. Light from the afternoon sun streamed through its stained-glass windows spilling rainbows onto the room's moss green carpet. I hopscotched circles of light as if jumping across a stream.

When I learned a new community was being built nearby, I put a deposit on a small cottage. Several months later, the developer returned my money explaining the "Garden Hamlet" project was "on hold." I'd sold the home where I'd raised my children, and the dream of living near the Sanctuary was no longer viable. So I purchased a 1950s ranch in a historic neighborhood in Hendersonville. With black walnut hardwood floors like none I'd ever seen and a vintage aqua tile bathroom, the house had a unique charm.

To those who ask why, after 15 years, I left that Druid Hills home, I say, "The house kicked me out."

Approaching 70, I'd toyed with the idea of downsizing, but was loath to leave. In spring, wild crocuses scattered by errant squirrels purpled the lawn. Greetings from bloodroot, green and gold, and trillium followed. From February, when daphne's white blooms perfumed the air, until October, when fuchsia anemones turned into puff balls, the yard was a riot of color and scents.

While living in that house, I'd healed from my divorce and buried my parents and only sister. In a room over the garage, cathedraled by four majestic oaks, I'd crafted poems and cataloged my father's World War II letters and diaries before sending them to the Smithsonian. But I'd also suffered from chronic sinus infections. Air quality tests identified the culprits: mildew and mold.

Immediately I shifted into overdrive. Every piece of fabric had to be cleaned or disposed of, every stick of furniture washed down. Books trashed or recycled. Walls swabbed and coated with mold-resistant paint. A humidifier installed in the crawl space.

After two grueling months, a voice began harping in my head: *The house is pristine now. Why not sell?*

I called my son, a real estate agent, and told him to list it.

Within days of that decision, a cottage that had been built when the Garden Hamlet project resumed came on the market. I decided to take a look. Walking into "Sunflower," I was drawn to south-facing windows that overlooked a pasture where goats grazed. In my excitement, I failed to register the animal heads mounted to the cottage walls—deer, elk, and moose—or the taxidermied rooster perched on a water stand. If I had, I might have backed right out of that place. Something shielded me from seeing those trophies, inviting me to stay.

Even though all the bedrooms were upstairs—not ideal for aging in place—I decided to buy it. The owner emptied my soon-to-be home of its rustic furniture and his hunting trophies but left a memento: an antler chandelier in the master bedroom. My son assured me that no moose were killed in the making of that light fixture, that antlers are shed. Even so, I hung sun catchers, Celtic crosses, pocket labyrinths, and party favors on it until I could replace it.

Through those same windows, I now watch bluebirds flit in and out of their box near my porch to feed their new brood. I scan the cottages that ring the pasture. Some appear empty, others occupied. Although designed as vacation rentals and second homes, almost a third now have permanent residents like me. When guests ask if the Garden Hamlet is an intentional community, I respond, "I hope someday."

On my walk, I pass a red barn, recently restored, and head toward the lake. When Catholics owned the property, they called the 30 acres of water Madonna Lake. The next owner changed the name back to Highland. A statue of the Blessed Mother, her foot on a snake, her palms open skyward, stands sentinel over a terraced lawn leading to the water. Campers once sat here in rows, watching skits and joining in sing-alongs. It still feels like her lake to me.

Finding Home

At the Sanctuary, staff are readying for a healer recently featured on a Netflix documentary. He is one of many spiritual teachers, integral theorists, and mind-body practitioners, who offer programs only footsteps away.

Finding home has been a journey. Each location where I've tarried offered a unique bundle of gifts. Highland Lake is no different and no place is forever. I will eventually move on. For now, however, I am at home here. And when I see children race to the fence to feed the goats, I head to the refrigerator, retrieve a bag of sliced apples and carrots, and go outside to join the fun. •

Copyright 2022, Karen Luke Jackson

Karen Luke Jackson, of Flat Rock, North Carolina, has authored two poetry collections, *The View Ever Changing* and *GRIT*, and her stories have appeared in journals and magazines, including *Reckon Review*, *Nobody's Home*, *moonShine review*, *Emrys Journal*, and *Town Magazine*. Karen also co-edited *The Story Mandala: Finding Wholeness in a Divided World*. A member of the North Carolina Writers' Network and the North Carolina Poetry Society, Karen draws inspiration from family stories, contemplative practices, nature, and clowning.

A Mountain and a Girl
by Jim Riggs

In 1957, a few dozen Iowa State College forestry students devoted our summer to studying in the Appalachian Mountains near Franklin, North Carolina. Arriving early, a buddy and I laced our boots at a trailhead for a ramble to Wayah Bald, a peak in the Nantahala National Forest. We hiked the picturesque old road that would become part of the Appalachian Trail. Near the peak, our overcast day changed. We emerged through the clouds to view a wrinkled white sea, a calm ocean, a magic carpet, with pointed peaks, like islands from underwater volcanoes rising like welcoming verdant respites. The white mantle transformed our perspective of the world, boosting our ardor for the day. The scene ranks high among my most treasured remembrances.

Being older now means opening my mind to such lovely memories. Recollections invade my brain. Images of North Carolina's beauty—that moment in the Appalachian Mountains and an instant with a charming young woman, both from my nineteenth summer—drift into my thoughts now on a Southern breeze.

The beauty of the moment that encouraged my spirit to step onto that magical carpet-cloud will forever be connected to the beauty of the Carolina girl who stepped away from that same trail earlier that morning. Loretta Fontaine's misfortune at forgetting her purse became my good fortune at a moment in my life.

Loretta's woven wicker handbag drowsed on a car-sized boulder, a shelf to rest on while she snapped a photo, perhaps. Inside was a wallet containing a driver's license with a picture of the pretty girl with dark hair, oval face, and bright dark eyes. Loretta was an attractive young woman. I was a young man with little experience involving the opposite sex, but certainly a growing interest.

On my North Carolina map, I charted a trip. My path to return Loretta's purse carried me over 75 miles of meandering mountain roads.

At a pay phone I dialed her number.

"Hello." It was her mother.

"My name is Jim Riggs. I'm a forestry student. I found Loretta's purse near Wayah Bald. I could take it to her on Saturday."

At camp, I thought about the pretty girl. Could I build a relationship? Might we have a day together? Or would I just do my good deed of returning her purse and drive home?

Saturday morning, I dressed in clean shorts, my best T-shirt, and beat-up tennis shoes. I turned my Chevy toward Hendersonville.

Two hours later, I filled my gas tank and asked directions to the Fontaine house. I drove through a mountain pass and turned into a long driveway to a stately home. My finger neared the doorbell. I began to lose my nerve.

At home, my bedroom contained a single bed, a small chest, and our water heater. Now, I stood in front of a mansion.

Mrs. Fontaine was tall, dressed in casual elegance. Her Southern charm exuded warmth.

I introduced myself. "Hi. Mrs. Fontaine? I'm Jim Riggs. I called about your daughter's purse, near Wayah Bald."

I handed her the purse and turned toward my car to drive back to Franklin, but Mrs. Fontaine insisted I stay.

"Just a moment, Jim. Come in. Sit down. Loretta will want to meet you."

I sat on her couch, surveying the spacious living room. The furniture and accessories dwarfed ours in Iowa.

A moment later, Loretta bounded down the stairs. This youngster glowed with her mother's charm. She thanked me for returning her purse. Her broad smile, dark flashing eyes, and round cheeks made her pretty now. I saw beauty on her horizon. She and her mother both steered the conversation toward my experiences at forestry camp and at Iowa State.

Her family was invited to spend the day at their neighbor's, they said, and they asked me to join them. I refused. They insisted I was welcome.

A Mountain and a Girl

Loretta and I and her friends spent much of our day at her friend's estate, swimming in their pool, frolicking in the water, sitting beside the pool, talking for hours. We talked about schools: my small-town Iowa high school in the North, her private segregated school in the South, and the Negro schools which Loretta insisted were as good as her white school.

"We even give them our old textbooks."

We ate a splendid Southern meal served by maids in black and white uniforms. They carried platters containing each course. Salt came in a silver bowl with a tiny spoon. I was in over my head—and I knew it.

In North Carolina, I left behind a mountain, a pretty girl, and forestry. I grow older now with memories of 38 years teaching mathematics and 61 years, so far, with a beautiful Iowa girl. •

Copyright 2022, Jim Riggs

Following his career teaching mathematics in Iowa, Jim Riggs settled near a beach in the mild climate of Hilton Head Island, South Carolina. He spends much of his time writing short stories and finishing his manuscript, "Fannie," creative biographical non-fiction about the life of his grandmother. His first novel, *Freedom Run*, drew rave reviews from readers.

His writing group, Island Writers Network, has given him opportunities to tune his stories during workshops and share his words at open mics. Jim's poetry and prose have appeared in three IWN anthologies.

Editor's note: "Loretta Fontaine" is a pseudonym to protect privacy.

November Wind
by Bob Amason

Orv and I were freshman-year roommates. Moving in that late summer day in 1970, we opened the door to our dorm room at Georgia Tech, and the Atlanta heat rushed out of the airless room like an evil, demonic being. We managed to get the small windows open and a box fan blowing. The fan merely drove the hot air faster.

Moments later we met Ray, our new neighbor. Two days later our fourth roomie, Bruce, joined us.

We four freshmen were inseparable. We attended an obligatory welcome presentation where a smug upperclassman invited us to look to our left and then to our right. He declared that only one of us would graduate. I didn't believe him. I should have.

I was proud of smuggling a small black-and-white television into the dorm and watching TV using an earphone. The illicit electronics was the big success of my freshman year. That is, unless you count the time when I willfully violated the laws of the State of Georgia regarding the purchase of alcohol by a minor. At 17, I already had a receding hairline accompanied by a Richard Nixon-quality five o'clock-shadow. Orv, Ray, and

Bruce all looked at me and chorused, "You're buying the hooch!"

That trio waited in the car while I trooped into the seedy-looking liquor store. Secretly quaking in fear of discovery as I loaded the cart to the gills, I reminded myself to casually say that I was 21 should I be challenged. Bottle of vodka, I'm 21; bottle of Bourbon, I'm 21; Six-pack? I'm 21. I made this a silent chant as I approached the checkout counter where a tired-looking fellow with pockmarked skin, thinning gray hair, stained teeth, and a cigarette dangling from his lower lip stood ready to assist me in the commission of my crime.

How does one get a lit cigarette to dangle from one's lower lip? I was still distractedly contemplating this unique talent when the cashier asked, "Anything else?"

"I'm 21!" I squeaked.

"Yeah, yeah, sure you're 21," the cigarette flicked with each word. "Anything else?"

"Nooope." I squeaked.

"Ok, that'll be $123.50."

My fingers shook as I handed over the cash and struggled the overloaded cart out the door.

"Come back anytime," said the dangling cigarette.

The rest of my freshman year was as ignominious as my cool manner in buying liquor underage. Orv, Ray, and Bruce all had GPAs in the 3-point-somethings. I hit a wall with freshman calculus. And despite conducting a couple legendary bacchanals under the very nose of our hall counselor, my freshman year was not characterized by an alcohol-induced haze. No, I faced it sober. Mostly.

And I sucked at school. At the end of November, leaning into in a freezing, eye-watering wind, I climbed "The Hill" at Georgia Tech to visit the math professor's office to find posted on his door my first failing grade—ever. I knew it would be an "F," but I had to walk up there and see it—in person.

And failure was far from being finished with me. Sophomore year dawned with an even worse performance, and I re-acquainted myself with the long, frigid November walk to see yet another "F" emblazoned next to my name. This time it was physics.

I took stock of myself and what I was trying to do. I made a commitment. I grew up. I clawed, scratched, sweated, and worked all hours to graduate at last with a degree from Georgia Tech—and on-time, too, if you don't count taking a couple summer quarters. That smug upperclassman's prediction of who would not graduate was eerily accurate. Only, I was surprised to be the last one standing. Of the four of us, I'm the one who should have been bagging groceries for a living. Instead, I got a master's degree from Georgia Tech and a PhD from the University of Florida. I was a successful U.S. Air Force officer and, I think, a fairly decent college professor.

November Wind

Ray graduated a year after I did. Bruce quit after freshman year. He married his high-school sweetheart, and they had a baby. I last saw Orv in 1973. He was leaning against his broken-down car in the emergency lane on I-75 a couple miles north of Macon. He turned down a ride.

We all made our choices.

Smart will only get you so far. Success is about getting out the shovel and digging yourself out of a hole regardless of the blisters, fear, sweat, and distractions. It's about leaning into the freezing November wind that blows failure in your face on a hill in Atlanta or anywhere you are headed.

Success takes all that and maybe, just for fun when you are young and stupid, buying illegal hooch with feigned aplomb from a guy with a cigarette dangling, in defiance of all physics, from his lower lip. •

Copyright 2022, Bob Amason

Bob Amason is a retired U.S. Air Force Lieutenant Colonel who was a college professor for 25 years. A member of the Florida Writer's Association, Bob writes under his pen name, Frank A. Mason. Bob is author of *The Journeyman Chronicles*, a series of novels about the adventures of a young master gunsmith caught up in the American Revolution. Bob Amason lives in St Augustine, Florida, with his overachieving wife who is a research professor and author of a forthcoming series of children's books.

This Much I Understand
by Wendy A. Miller

We five women living in a country foreign to each of us and who did not speak the same language found each other when we needed finding. This much, I understand.

When the Air Force assigned my husband to a rural region of Belgium, I vowed to improve my high school French out of respect for my host country. Twice a week for three years, I dodged semi-trucks hauling sugar beets on a two-lane highway to attend French class 40-minutes away at an international military base in Mons.

Arriving safely for that first class, I stepped into a classroom filled with a collection of students from different countries—most were military or family members, and some were corporate civilians. What we had in common was our inability to understand each other. A stooped man with scruffs of gray hair stood out because of his advanced age. I'd see him walking after class, prompting me to point to my car and ask, "Would you like a ride?" He looked to the sun and declined. I asked again on a rainy day, and I was not surprised when he nodded.

This Much I Understand

He did not speak English, and I did not speak Spanish, so we tried to communicate in toddler French, but his thick accent made him doubly difficult for me to understand. I could not understand the directions for his home, so he pointed to the commissary on the base. I dropped him in front of the coffee shop and watched his slow, bent gait disappear inside. It became our routine for me to drive him on the days it drizzled. Each time, he repeated words I understood to mean I reminded him of his daughter. I smiled and nodded. Later, I learned I'd misunderstood.

Each semester, my class had a new mix of students. After the summer break, a slender woman about my age with an engaging smile I had not had in class before approached me. She confirmed I was the woman who'd given the aged man a ride. Through our rudimentary shared French, she explained she was his daughter-*in-law* and that, sadly, he'd passed away. She went on to say that he'd spoken of me. To my shock, her father-in-law had understood me perfectly. The daughter-in-law knew I had a 4-year-old son, as did she, and our husbands were both military officers. I understood then he'd been trying to connect us because she and I had much in common.

From then on, before class, she and I worked to chit-chat in our shared language—like her father-in-law, she did not speak English. Seeing our interest in small talk, a classmate from Romania invited us and two other classmates, one from Germany and the other from Japan, to her home to practice French. The five of us met once a week and vowed only to talk in French, which required lots of gesturing and giggles.

Our curiosity about each other kept the conversation flowing. We did not speak of it, but the War in Afghanistan raged. The military wives among us understood that shared worry without needing words. All of us mothers—Germany pregnant with her first—desired a better world. Somehow, learning a language and finding friendships beyond our borders seemed to move us towards that goal.

I looked forward to our time together. We did not have the vocabulary to go deep, so I felt free to show my silly side, singing, off-key, a children's folk song I learned in high school French. As our friendships grew, we relied on each other for favors. I purchased items at the American commissary they could not buy, or sometimes I translated English. Our German friend volunteered to watch our family beagle for a few days. I warned her he was naughty, often getting into trash cans. When we returned, I sheepishly asked what he'd done. She reassured me he'd been well-behaved and said, "Perhaps he understands German better than English."

I invited the women and their families to my house during the holidays. Each guest brought a dish from her respective country. Japan created an artistic sushi Christmas tree. Germany tantalized our sugar cravings with homemade cookies. Spain arrived two hours late carrying a frittata—we laughed when she said, "Six is too early for a party. Eight is almost bearable." Even a freak power outage did not damage the jovial spirit. Romania helped me sprinkle the room with candles. The following week, my friends teased me, saying, "*Quelle fête romantique!*

This Much I Understand

Years and other life experiences have dimmed my recollection of those days, but I remember their voices and the earnestness of our attempts to communicate with each other, to share our lives as they were then. We came together at a time when we all needed uplifting, and discovered we were more alike than different.

This much, I understand. •

Copyright 2022, Wendy A. Miller

Wendy A. Miller is a member of Taste Life Twice Writers. Her work has appeared in three previous Personal Story Publishing Project anthologies and on "6-Minute Stories" podcasts. *Star 82 Review, Tiny Seed Journal, Grown and Flown,* and more have published her essays and poetry. When she isn't writing, she is on the fairways or meandering among Douglas fir trees near her home in Oregon, where she lives with her husband of 30 years and her son when he is home from college. View her work at www.wendyamiller.com or on Twitter @WendyAMiller35.

Signposts
by Annie McLeod Jenkins

I've always been a linear girl who does not like change. At age four, I cried and cried about the removal of a tree in our front yard. As a child, I never wanted new pajamas. To this day, discarding an old shirt or pair of jeans makes me feel like I'm betraying a friend. I love "to-do" lists because they help me see the framework of the day. I like predictability.

In my early 20s, I did step out of this comfort zone, quitting a teaching job and heading west with a friend in an ancient Volkswagen Squareback, loaded to the windowsills with our worldly goods. We each had $200 in grub stake, a vague notion about Colorado ski mountains, and the names of friends and family from Memphis to Oklahoma to Denver. Ultimately, following the advice of Denver friends, we ended up in Steamboat Springs, Colorado, working as waitresses and living in a former bunkhouse on a local ranch.

By the spring of 1972, after a full season of living hand-to-mouth, skiing every day, keeping my earnings in a sock in my dresser drawer, and doing no more planning than whether to sleep on the benches in the restaurant's bar or drive the

25 miles back to the bunkhouse, I was ready for more stability. Out of the blue, I was offered a job at my alma mater in North Carolina, Salem College. Crazily, perhaps, I turned it down, because as much as I wanted a retirement plan, I was not going back east. This decision might have been influenced by knowledge that my parents were not happy about a man I was dating, plus by my youthful determination to choose my own path.

In the meantime, my sidekick decided to get married to her French-Canadian boyfriend (another story) and move to god-knows-where. I forged on toward some stability, but without giving in to my parents. I applied for a teaching job in nearby Oak Creek, to begin in the fall of 1972. However, my friend owned our car, and then the car died. I could not afford a car, but I needed a car—a 4-wheel drive car, at that. Furthermore, I discovered that I would be required to live in the Oak Creek district in order to teach there. Oak Creek was a long-dead mining town with a colorful but seedy history. I did not want to live there; so, on the rutted desolate road to a played-out town, I hit another roadblock.

Still determined to stay in Colorado and needing some time to consider my options, I moved briefly to Denver, followed by a few weeks driving through Mexico (fodder for another story). Upon my return to civilization, I found a letter from my family, alerting me that my mother needed an operation. I felt compelled to visit South Carolina for her surgery and recovery, still planning to return to Colorado to find "serious work."

Temporarily back at my parents' home, I answered the telephone one morning to hear a vaguely familiar voice say, "Annie, this is Edith Kirkland in the Admissions Office at Salem. We heard you were back on the East Coast (That's quite a grapevine, Salem College!), and since the job here is still available, we wondered if you would reconsider." I was beginning to feel that the universe had a message for me. As I saw it, I had two problems: caving-in to my parents' wishes and having to move back east. The first problem was the hardest to swallow.

I felt so conflicted. I could see that taking the job at Salem made sense, but I was determined that my parents not think that I had made the choice because of their urging. Childish? Yes. Easy to overcome? No.

Eventually, I took my dilemma to a trusted advisor and minister. To his credit, he did not go all sanctimonious on me and say, "When God shuts a door, He opens a window." Using secular language, he advised me to look for signposts. He suggested that if I kept seeing a particular signpost, no matter which road I followed, then perhaps I should pay attention.

I took the job at Salem College, which I enjoyed for 11 years—ten more years than I had signed for. The job was tailor-made for me, offering much of what I had loved about teaching, with none of the downsides. I adored my working conditions, my co-workers, and the mission. No longer did I keep my earnings in a sock, and I gained a 401K. During my time employed there, I fell in love, got married, had two children, and found a life that I adored, right back in the "briar patch."

Life can be an uncertain and winding road, but signposts can be our friends—if we pay attention. •

Copyright 2022, Annie McLeod Jenkins

Annie McLeod Jenkins lives in Winston-Salem, North Carolina, and is a dues-paying but inactive member of Winston-Salem Writers. Long retired but still sometimes tired, she enjoys the pace of life in her 70s. She finds it easy to fill a day by getting up, reading the paper, preparing some meals, walking, reading, sometimes gardening, and giving advice to her adult children and husband. Four of her stories have appeared in collections of the Personal Story Publishing Project.

Heart and Soul
by Bill Donohue

Our son Jeremy moved with syncopated success through the years of early intervention, various therapists, and the elementary and middle school hurdles that face all students with "special needs." He was typically sweet and mischievous for someone with Down syndrome, short in stature, cognitively challenged, but making his—and our—journey both routinely inspirational and also a daily challenge.

Following two previous pioneers at West Forsyth High School, Jeremy became the football team's "spirit coach," helping the trainer and mostly hanging with the team. Having "big" friends was something we had identified early as a key to his social acceptance. Being around popular cheerleaders was a real plus.

Looking for other opportunities to develop more acceptance and high school belonging, we asked the school principal if he thought Jeremy could be in the school play. He already enjoyed the school's inclusive "Introduction to Theater" class. With the mirrored frown of experience, the principal said, "We have 2,000 students here and at least three dozen parents think their child is ready for Broadway. I'd look somewhere else." *Ouch*.

Two days later we, by chance, ran into the drama teacher. Undaunted by the previous advice, Jeremy's mother, gently inquired, "Mr. Rushton, we see that you have an all-school musical on the calendar. Do you think there is any way Jeremy might be able to help backstage with sets or props or something?"

"No, I don't think that's going to be possible," came the quick and definitive reply, as he turned his back to us. It was rude, it stung. We took a quick breath, preparing to offer a plea when he spun on his heels with a huge smile saying, "Jeremy is going to be too busy preparing to be a "Jet" in *West Side Story*!!"

Weeks later Jeremy was handed his bright blue "Jet's" jacket and assigned the role of "Fidget." We raced to the video and then to the script, flying through credits, looking everywhere for "Fidget." Mr. Rushton not only gave Jeremy a chance to fully express himself, he had created a new character for Jeremy to embody it!

Three years later at the senior awards ceremony, with a thousand proud parents and as many students in attendance, the last award of the evening was announced. A new theater teacher had since replaced Mr. Rushton and began her remarks slowly, "This year's award recipient was not the star nor the lead in any of our productions these past four years, but he was the heart and soul of every musical we performed." With the announcement of "Jeremy," the audience erupted in applause and rose to their feet.

Would that Jeremy could rise as easily—always.

The pulmonologist said it was a real close one. "We almost lost him!" Draining six liters of fluid from his lungs from aspiration pneumonia and later surgically removing the thick coating that choked those lungs had numbed us against reality.

Jeremy had soared with his independence as a young man with Down syndrome. After a four-year, inclusive, residential experience at University of North Carolina-Greensboro's "Beyond Academics" program, he moved into an apartment and got a job as greeter at a nearby Japanese restaurant. With social services supports, he continued to blossom and soon became engaged, envisioning a home and family life of his own. His fiancé and he offered communion at church, shared a weekly book club with peers, and enjoyed all the Special Olympics events their time could allow.

But at a summer church camp for people with disabilities, he developed the pneumonia that would send him racing to the hospital. While his Down syndrome always represented concerns, his later diagnosis of FSH-Muscular Dystrophy loomed as the real threat.

This second neuro-muscular disease meant that typical muscle deterioration was obvious, but more subtle came diminished vocal strength, hearing, and breathing. Not only had his Special Olympics and para-karate competition declined, but as part of his hospitalization, Jeremy further lost his ability to swallow. Overnight, he became a "tube feeder."

Two years later, his resilience shows, bringing his mom evening tea and stubbornly planning our family dinner. He yearns for

Heart and Soul

the pandemic's end, ready to return to his restaurant. He tolerates relentless day-feeding and evening pump routines in a way we can hardly imagine, with unabashed public acceptance of his circumstances and who he is in them.

Covid and finances have the marriage on hold. Church and book club are mostly virtual; sports complicated—but all bring joy and belonging with friends.

Under Medicaid Supported Living he is back to his own "residence with support." His "Home-and-Community-Based" provider and her son share his rent and gregarious lifestyle apart from us. We cherish the energy, fun, and familiar comfort he brings on occasional visits.

Jeremy remains heart and soul. •

Copyright 2022, Bill Donohue

Bill Donohue is a disability advocate living in Winston Salem. Most of his writing (ncwaiveractionteam.com) informs and prods legislative inertia for the 15,000 with Developmental Disabilities waiting a decade or more for services while potential caregivers struggle for a living wage. Bill's first novel is a family's saga with early onset dementia, chronicled in *The Kind of September*, Amazon (2013).

Christmas 1970
by Rosemary James

A chill in the air, Christmas approaching, everybody excited, but me. I learned the real meaning of Christmas in church. I felt guilty for my anger and sadness during a beautiful season celebrating the birth of Jesus. The only gift I wanted was for my mother to return for us and never leave again.

Aunt Bea, my mother's sister-in-law, busied herself making a cheerful setting for the holiday. A spruce tree cut from the family farm stood in its new place, the living room. A huge tree, homemade ornaments, and paper-chain garland adorned the branches. Aunt Bea spent hours showing and helping her son Tommy, my sisters and brothers, all younger, and me how to make our first Christmas ornaments. The tree had no lights, but it was lovely. I felt proud of our ornaments. We stood back and admired them.

That 1970 Christmas, nothing brightened my sadness, not even the kid's joy when boxes wrapped in shiny, colorful foil paper with a huge bow arrived in the mail. I watched my brothers open their gifts. Dougie and Ricky tore the blue paper in strips. Glenn ripped his in large pieces.

Christmas 1970

"I gotta dump truck. Look Dougie," Glenn yelled.

Dougie, tearing at his paper, "Wow. A bull dozier."

"What'd ya get Ricky," Glenn asked.

I helped pull the remaining paper loose from Ricky's box.

"Cars! Cars!" Ricky squealed holding the hauler truck loaded with tiny vehicles in the air.

The boys rolled the play equipment across the living room floor with great passion. I saw the big-boy dreams in their gleaming eyes. "Rmm, Rmm," little voices pretended.

Phyllis and Debby hugged their matching dolls, one with a light blue dress, the other pale-yellow. Both had short brown hair with bangs, white socks and shoes, blue eyes with closing eye lids. They pretended to feed, diaper, walk, then rock their babies to sleep. I was tempted to tear the shiny red paper from my present. But I held strong. I loved Mommy for sending the gift, but I wouldn't enjoy it until she came home.

"Sissy, why ain't ya opening your gift," Aunt Bea asked.

"Don't feel like it right now. I'm watching the kids have fun." Partially true. I knew by the size and shape of the package my gift was a doll. The angry side of me said I didn't need a doll to feed, diaper, walk, or soothe to sleep. I'd had plenty of practice doing that with my younger brothers. As far back as my 8-year-old memory took me I'd always been helping Mom care for babies.

The first letter we received from my mother since her months in prison was enclosed in the box.

> Hi kids,
> Merry Christmas! I hope y'all enjoy your gifts. I wanted each of you to have something special. There's a job program here, they pay us to work. I saved my money to buy y'all Christmas presents.
>
> I know mommy has been gone from y'all a lot. I miss each of you. When I get home, we'll go swimming and do fun things together.
>
> Phyllis and Debby do you like kindergarten? I hope you're learning lots. Sissy, do you like second grade as much as the first grade. I bet its hard work, but you can do it. Glenn, you help Aunt Bea watch your brothers while the girls are in school. You're a big boy now.
>
> I love and miss y'all very much. I want to hug and kiss each of you). I'll be back home soon. Be good and mind Uncle Kookie and Aunt Bea.
>
> Love,
> Mommy
>
> Sissy, I know you're being a good helper to Aunt Bea with the kids. I'll be home soon, and never leave you

Christmas 1970

again. I promise you. We'll get another house by ourselves when I come home. I love you, my big girl and helper. Mommy

I read the letter to the kids with Aunt Bea's help sounding out some words, except my part. I didn't want my brothers and sisters to hear Mom's promise. She always breaks her promises. I love my mommy and miss her, but she hurts us. I didn't know much about my daddy anymore. The last time I saw him he brought us back from a short visit with him to Granny Green's house. He doesn't come see us or write us.

It was difficult getting the kids to settle down at bedtime. Each little voice wanted to talk about how much they loved their gift and Mommy. Weary eyes, warm hearts, and carefree minds drifted off to sleep as I spoke a fairy tale of happily-ever-after over them. I prayed for God to bring my mother home to us for good. To make my pretend story real, to be happy. •

Copyright 2022, Rosemary James

Rosemary V. James, a proud Appalachian woman from Estill County, currently lives in Richmond, Kentucky. She retired as an Occupational Therapist. Her joy in life is her eight grandchildren. After the passing of her husband, Rosemary began writing in 2019 through the Carnegie Center for Literacy and Learning in Lexington, graduating from its Author Academy. She is writing a socially informed memoir on the impact of child abuse and domestic violence across one's life. Read "Fly On" at opentohope.com. Her story "Firkins" appears in the PSPP anthology *Curious Stuff*.

Love in the Clouds
by Phyllis Castelli

The road wending up to the Blue Ridge Parkway near Mount Mitchell was curvy and hold-your-breath steep. My husband, Tom, drove with great care and patience as our car corkscrewed up and around Singecat Ridge towards Buck Creek Gap and the Parkway entrance.

Tom and I were reconciling again, falling in love again, trying to stitch our marital crazy quilt back together. For us, true love and marriage were never easily fitted pieces. We both deeply loved the North Carolina mountains, so we headed west from Winston-Salem early that morning with hopeful hearts.

We were bone tired, worn down from our chaotic lives. I remember the sense of relaxing into being together and feeling the problems fall away, like stones rolling down the mountainside. As we drove in attentive travel up the mountain, life at home faded into the background. Our world became nothing but the two of us and the lush green views in the distance.

Smoky mist soon enveloped the massive, majestic mountains. A steady, pounding rain began to fall. Dark, swirling clouds created a sense of seclusion and separation from the workaday world. We seemed to be floating upward to the point of Creation.

It was still pouring rain as we turned towards Craggy Gardens, our planned stop for lunch. As we drove through Craggy Pinnacle Tunnel, the shelter allowed a moment of complete silence, like taking a deep breath. As if on cue when we exited, the heavy rain turned to drizzle, then blue sky, leaving a clean-washed morning on the mountain. Our happiness made the picnic five-star delicious and felt like a first date. We dined surrounded by the sparkle of rain-fresh purple rhododendron.

After lunch, we headed north to Mount Mitchell State Park, a half-hour's drive through the Pisgah National Forest, followed by a snail's pace climb to the summit. Nothing east of the Mississippi was higher but the sky.

Mount Mitchell presided over a spruce-fir forest dark enough to warrant the name Black Mountains. Sadly, many areas had withered in the toxic environment of acid rain. Hundreds of trees stood gray and bare like old arthritic fingers pointing blame at the clouds. Standing with Tom facing such devastation, I made a silent vow to take better care of our marital environment.

Looking out for endless miles over the lower landscape was a lesson in perspective, in the smallness of humanity. From where we stood on the overlook, homes and barns below us lay like toys strewn in the grass. Our day-to-day homelife seemed very far away, with the juggled pressures of work, money, and dramatic teenagers no longer front and center. Tom took my hand, rekindling the strong love that first brought us together. I remembered the words of our favorite marriage prayer: "Help us to apply this love in practical things, so nothing divides us."

We walked to the park museum and read that Mount Mitchell was named for Elisha Mitchell, a 19th-century geology professor at the University of North Carolina. The State hired him to measure the elevation of the Black Mountains. Although he knew the mountains well, he fell to his death in 1857. I imagined the grief of his wife, Maria, who had been awaiting Elisha's safe return to Chapel Hill. Their story was a heartbreaking reminder for us to safeguard our time together.

Beyond the museum was the viewing platform, where Tom and I stood for a while, looking out in awe. Clouds surrounded us gently and then passed on like a kind thought, or a smile from a stranger. He pulled me close. I kissed him in the cloud "right there in front of God and everybody," as my grandmother would have said, chuckling that we had misbehaved.

On the way back from the look-out, we passed a young family. The mother said to her daughter, "Did you get that cloud? Now, put it in your pocket!" The little girl opened up her pocket and stuffed it in, like trying to save a handful of magic. I wondered if I could carry love in my pocket the same way.

Needing to start the journey home but reluctant to lose our sense of sanctuary, we sat talking in the grass with mugs of coffee as if we had no place to be but there. The late

Love in the Clouds

afternoon brightened. Sun and soft fog danced around us as the weather cleared. Tom stood, looking around thoughtfully.

"Today has been a good day," he said, and pulled me to my feet. "Let's go home."

When at last we headed down the mountain, the first fragment of a rainbow appeared. As we circled around in descent, more and more ribbons of bright color came into view until the entire perfect arc was ours, a blessing following the storm. •

Copyright 2022, Phyllis Castelli

Phyllis Castelli returned to her North Carolina hometown, Henderson, after retiring from her music career. She loves to spend time with her lifetime special interests: writing, music, photography, a pollinator garden, and Black Labrador Retrievers. Phyllis is interested in creating projects that knit together the beauty of all those favorites. Phyllis's poems and essays have appeared in *Quillkeepers Press*, *The Avocet*, *Scarlet Leaf Review*, and *Tar River Poets*, among others. As a very young poet, she published *Gentle, I Think*, a book of poems with pen and ink illustrations.

The Befuddled Entrepreneur
by Valerie Macon

It was that restless yearning for rite of passage (a driver's license) and the need for cash to fund his dream car (a red Camaro) that caused my son, Jeromy, just turned 15, to rethink, reorganize, and revitalize his dormant business venture, *Jeromy's Pet, Plant, and Premise Care Service*. To him, the timing seemed just right: the holiday season, people leaving town. He would lovingly care for their dogs and cats, water their plants, and even cut their lawns, if needed.

He was swift and sure in his resolve, as he usually was when he had a mind to do something. He designed an eye-catching flyer promising pet owners peace of mind when they leave town knowing that their pets, plants, and premises would be left in his competent hands. He developed an impressive data-gathering form and designed an eye-catching shirt with his business logo—a contented canine wearing a blissful smile. As I watched him take off on his bike to stuff 200 flyers in neighborhood mailboxes, I was impressed by his dedication to purpose.

The results were immediate. Even before he delivered his last brochure, the phone rang. It was a Mr. Jones, asking questions, wanting his services. Soon, arrangements were made to watch his two Shetland Collies, Shep and Lulu, while he and Mrs. Jones left town for the week. I drove Jeromy to Mrs. Jones' house and waited as she filled out his comprehensive data form. Everything seemed in order.

When Friday evening arrived, Jeromy put on his neon-yellow logo shirt and enlisted Dad to chauffeur him to the Jones' residence. Confident and professional in his approach, he entered the home of his first customer. Only minutes passed, however, before he appeared back at Dad's car, his brow troubled.

"I can't find the dog food anywhere," he complained. Moved by Jeromy's anxiety, Dad follows him into the house to help him find the missing chow. Together they make an exhaustive but fruitless search of the kitchen and other possible areas. Jeromy rereads his data sheet outlining detailed feeding instructions left by the fastidious Joneses, but the dog food is simply not where it is supposed to be. Befuddled, Jeromy decides to call them.

After two attempts at dialing the long-distance number on his data sheet and twice reaching the wrong number, Dad offers to dial for his rattled son. He picks up the phone to dial the number, and to his astonishment, there is a man on the other end of the line.

"Who is this?" the man questions sharply.

Dad states his name.

"What are you doing in my house?" the man barks.

Dad attempts to explain. But Mr. Jones, who it turns out has not left town, explains that he is calling to talk to Mrs. Jones, who, he warns, is due home any minute.

Now Jeromy and Dad feel like criminals and intruders who will likely terrify the unsuspecting Mrs. Jones. They plan a hasty retreat, but Shep and Lulu have other plans. They want to play hide-and-seek and take off running at reckless speed, darting under furniture, zigzagging in and out of rooms. Frantically, Dad and Jeromy scramble to catch the playful duo to put them back outside where they rightfully belong. But the dogs rip like lightening up the stairs and into forbidden territory where their pursuers feel increasingly uncomfortable. After a prolonged and harrowing chase, Shep and his sidekick, Lulu, are at last secured and herded outside. The interlopers, breathless and sweating, lock up and flee the scene.

Back at home, Jeromy paces the floor, trying to collect his thoughts and assesses the damage. He tells me how he and his dad have been racing around in the Jones' house. How he made two long-distance phone calls on their phone (he was more worried about this than anything else). All he could do now is call them and try to explain and to apologize.

Reaching their message mailbox, he makes two muddled attempts at wording a coherent message of what just happened. Frustrated, he gives up. He says, "What else could go wrong today?"

The Befuddled Entrepreneur

Just then, the phone rings. It is Mrs. Jones. She is calling to apologize that she had given Jeromy the wrong date. They would not be leaving town until tomorrow night.

Jeromy sighs as he collapses onto the couch, exhausted after his first day in business.

Jeromy is now a grown man. Apparently undeterred by his shaky beginnings in business, he has become a successful entrepreneur, owner of a coffee shop/restaurant and a food truck. He drives his latest dream car, a Corvette Z51, and he continues to talk about his next business venture.

He owns no pets. •

Copyright 2022, Valerie Macon

Valerie Macon calls Fuquay-Varina, North Carolina, home. Her poetry has appeared in *Kakalak*, *Whispers*, *Vision & Voice*, *Red Clay Review*, *Visions International*, *Clockhouse Review*, *Poetry in Plain Sight*, as well as numerous anthologies. She has authored five books of poetry: *Shelf Life*, *Sleeping Rough*, *A String of Black Pearls*, *The Shape of Today*, and *Page Turner*. She writes for Suburban Living Magazine.

Telling Eyes
by Suzanne Cottrell

I had my eyes set on teaching history, like my mom. History was interesting, familiar, and comforting. But when I completed my master's degree, teaching positions in history were scarce. Rather than abandon my desire to teach, I accepted available opportunities. Although my stomach knotted each time I switched to teaching a different subject area, my parents' divorce necessitated my working full time. I had to pay bills, including my student loan.

Wilson County Technical Institute offered me two part-time positions—teaching social sciences and pre-vocational classes for women. As a newlywed at age 24, I wondered if I could relate to these older, mostly single mothers, who lacked basic life skills such as balancing a checkbook, but I figured I could use some practice, too. I greeted them with "happy to see you" and a jittery smile, but they muffled their hellos with downcast eyes, avoiding glances. They sniffled some as they shared their stories of unplanned pregnancies, abusive relationships, or caring for siblings. As I listened to their challenges, my heart ached for them, but my mind dredged up memories of my parents' loud arguments, slamming doors, and childhood nightmares of separation. Self-doubt shadowed me.

Telling Eyes

During graduate school, I had denied my anger and insecurity over my parents' divorce. My weekly conversations with them were choppy sentences spoken through gritted teeth with forced restraint, resulting in tears and nausea. Caught between my mom and my dad, I refused to take sides.

My frozen teacher-smile did not diminish my concern for the women's hardships or my anguish over my parents' divorce. We helped each other as we shared stories, fears, and revealed our vulnerabilities. Our suppressed feelings bubbled to the surface. After my initial hesitation, I spoke for their benefit and for mine. "You can do this. You're strong," I said. *I can do this. I am strong.* They received my words with damp eyes and reluctant but courageous smiles. They faced their obstacles bravely. I faced mine, too, with the support of my husband. As the weeks progressed, our daily end-of-class departures included hugs and head-raised smiles. Our eyes connected and radiated some confidence. New friendships emerged through honest and meaningful interactions.

Throughout my schooling, I had struggled with another issue. Although I loved reading, my eyes refused to work together, causing double vision and blurriness. The print jumped on the page. This eye strain limited my reading to 20-minute sessions. *Am I going blind?* My chest would tighten when a teacher asked me to read aloud or to answer a reading comprehension question. I would shift in my seat, losing my place in the text, while praying she'd call on someone else. Clenched fists dug fingernails into my palms while I blinked and squinted to focus my eyes—and my life. Perhaps my adult students, dealing with their frustrations and fears, had similar experiences in school.

Indeed, the successes of my pre-vocational students motivated me. How they overcame the deficits in their life skills encouraged me to explore learning strategies to address my reading problem. The teacher became a student again. I returned to graduate school to train as a special education teacher.

From new research, my optometrist diagnosed my visual stress as Meares-Iren Syndrome, a perceptual processing disorder. Simply changing the lens color of my reading glasses to rose provided greater contrast and made reading easier for longer periods. My eyes dampened with happy tears. *If only I had known this earlier.*

I wanted to apply my new knowledge and to empower children with proven strategies to compensate for their learning disabilities. Helping reduce their anxiety and frustration while affording them learning opportunities would boost their self-esteem. Circumstances carried me to the Wake County Public School System, where I taught special needs children for 27 years. I built rapport with my students by asking about their interests and hobbies, as well as implementing relevant and engaging activities. The annual fishing field trip for my elementary students was a highlight. I smiled with thumbs up, capturing their eeks when they caught their first blue gills and recalling my fishing adventures with my family at a neighbor's farm pond. My students' eyes gleamed when they mastered "regrouping" in math, an "aha" moment. Each time one of my students read a chapter book independently, my eyes brightened. Besides building academic skills, we learned conflict resolution. I, too, needed to work out disputes rather than avoid them.

Telling Eyes

My students' needs propelled me to earn my National Board Professional Teaching Certification and to remain in the special education field. Together we learned patience, perseverance, and assertiveness. I saw myself in a different light and could erase some long-standing insecurity. I could see my students did too. •

Copyright 2022, Suzanne Cottrell

Suzanne Cottrell, a member of Taste Life Twice Writers, Creative Voices, and NC Writers' Network, lives with her husband in Granville County, North Carolina. An outdoor enthusiast and retired teacher, she enjoys reading, writing, knitting, hiking, Pilates, and yoga. Her prose has appeared in numerous journals and anthologies, including five Personal Story Publishing Project anthologies, three Prolific Press anthologies, *Dragon Poet Review*, *Dual Coast Magazine*, *Parks and Points*, and *Nailpolish Stories*. She's the author of three poetry chapbooks: *Gifts of the Seasons, Autumn and Winter ; Gifts of the Seasons, Spring and Summer* ; and *Scarred Resilience* (Kelsay Books). www.suzanneswords.com

New Trajectory
by R.V. Kuser

Like most people, when I was young, I imagined what job I might like to have. I thought about what I could do as a grown-up. The possibilities to be considered were endless. For a child, the world is a place without limits, open to whatever we can think of doing.

One of the reasons many children dream about all kinds of interesting jobs has to do with the support they receive from teachers, peers, and, most importantly, their family. Families provide crucial support to generate a spark of interest in their child's mind. It is the idea that you can do anything if you put your mind to it.

Growing up, I was not as fortunate as some other children. I had a grandiose idea of acquiring a great job, which would also mean going to college. But when I spoke to my parents about the kind of job I wanted to pursue, they reacted with silence. They thought I was kidding. I felt bewildered and dismayed. Why would my parents not acknowledge my enthusiasm about going to college and having a great job?

My parents explained that because of my learning disability, I was better suited to landscaping work.

I felt very hurt and confused for a number of reasons, starting with how they weren't considering my opinion on the matter. While I enjoyed some aspects of landscaping, I did not want it for a career. My disability was always mentioned first whenever I was doing projects or applying for a job. I saw a very interesting contradiction. When I was very young, I had some physical problems that were related to cognitive issues.
My parents found a specialist who generated strategies to help me to stand and walk on my own without any other support. My parents told me there was nothing I could not do, even with a learning disability. Yet here, in this situation, I was being told that I was too slow or disabled to go to college.

I thought that since I was not going to college, I could possibly help other people in the learning-disabled community to read, write, and do math. After I learned about an adult education program that taught people with learning disabilities, I signed up for volunteer work. My job was to give any assistance that I could to the students. Some of the students were my age, and some were older. It was very sad because none of the students was getting any noticeable attention.

I was paired with a man named Frank. He was 5' 5," average weight, and probably in his mid-40s. He also looked very tired. I assured him that I was there to help him. We spent time talking about anything and everything. Later, I found out that Frank did not like to talk too much. He told me that most of his life, he felt that he could not do anything right.

"What can we work on right now?" I asked Frank.

After a long hesitation, he replied, "Math is not good."

I began to work with him to help discover new tools to unlock for him the mystery of mathematics. I began by pushing aside his math book. He looked very surprised when I moved his book.

"What are you doing? You can't do that."

I brought "manipulatives" out to help him. Manipulatives are shapes that can be handled to represent numbers when teaching math. The manipulatives helped him to "see and feel" the math problems he was working on. At the same time, I asked him questions to help him feel as though he were teaching me. We worked through a math problem together.

I said to him, "You did a great job; you found the answer by yourself!" He smiled and his sleepy eyes opened up wide. He was surprised and pleased. And he was without words. Then a smile evolved into even a bigger smile. By the end of the evening, he was able to understand subtraction and addition problems. Frank had discovered something he never knew before, understood the world in a way that changed everything.

After seeing Frank make such great progress in our first meeting, I realized that I had been successful even without any formal experience in teaching. I knew right then that I was going to be a non-certified schoolteacher. This moment generated a whole new trajectory for how I thought about myself and how I might help others. Even though I was Frank's teacher, he taught me a valuable lesson. Never again would I question my ability in the same way when it came to teaching.

"I can do anything" became not only my firm belief, it is what I wanted to teach others to believe about themselves. •

Copyright 2022, R.V. Kuser

R.V. Kuser lives in Winston Salem, North Carolina. He is an advocate, educator, motivational speaker, consultant, and author of two books. He is also a Southeast ADA (American with Disabilities Act) Trainer Member. R.V. is on a lifelong quest for ways to overcome misperceptions about individuals living with disabilities, to let everyone know we CAN do anything. With his wife, Marlene, they both give a greater insight when speaking publicly and advocating. They would love to hear from you—questions, comments, or just to say "hello." Contact them at kusertalk.com.

Make It Through
by Leigh Ann Whittle

If you had stepped into our pediatrician's office one spring afternoon in 2021, you would have seen a woman seeking solutions for her toddler's skin allergies. Other than the boy's "itching" desire to scratch his irritated limbs, you may have thought it was just late on a mundane Monday for the pair. You probably would not have imagined that the woman had received a phone call less than an hour before with a message she could not fathom receiving:

"Your biopsy results are in.
I'm sorry to say you have cancer."

A dreaded phone call. *The* dreaded phone call. And yet, here I was at 41, mother of two children under 5, receiving that call.

Three days later, I sat in another doctor's office. My oncologist informed me that my breast cancer would require chemotherapy and a mastectomy. After she left the exam room, I sat processing the news. My nurse navigator, a woman I had met about 15 minutes before, sat next to me. On her lap were the notes she took while the oncologist spoke. I did not want the notes. Having my treatment plan in writing made it too real. After all, I was briefly and unwittingly placed in someone else's life or trapped in a horrible dream, right?

Soon, I was crying. My tears were not over the severity of treatment or even the loss of hair or a body part I would ultimately experience. The tears were for my family. I could not bear the thought of putting them through cancer. They did not deserve this. But none of us had a choice. Cancer was the cross we were meant to bear.

I learned many lessons through my cancer journey, enough to fill several volumes. One most significant lesson is "demonstrating resilience."

Life abounds with mis-directions and the unexpected. I have seen my share. My life experiences, each one and all together, contributed to how I responded to cancer. As I walked through this particular "season," my mind returned to the years we spent wanting to build a family before our first child was born. That experience showed me blue skies wait for those who persevere, who survive the storm. Recollections of that season provided comfort, showing me that just as I made it through unexplained infertility, I would make it through cancer.

"Make it through." That phrase sounds a bit detached, as if going through a challenging experience is like simply passing through a tunnel. I stay at home with my young children, but I spent six days tethered to an IV pole at the hospital. Does "make it through" effectively capture the feeling that I was failing my children because I could not be present for them while I was taking my treatments? Those mornings I spent standing in my backyard, running my fingers through my hair, watching tufts of it fly into the breeze, telling myself that some bird was using that hair for its home—was that considered how I would "make it through"? Did the promise that I would "make it through" ease the pain of breaking my husband's heart with my diagnosis, knowing I had absolutely no control over the situation?

Being resilient is neither easy nor painless. Facing cancer is also neither easy nor painless. I resolved that I may have *had* cancer, but cancer did not *have* me. If I were to "make it through," I would need to adopt a resilient attitude.

And I did. Six rounds of chemotherapy, 12 additional rounds of immunotherapy, and two surgeries in a 61-week span from diagnosis to final treatment resulted in me becoming cancer-free. As I transition into survivorship, I feel like a butterfly emerging from a chrysalis—certainly changed, perhaps stronger, and hopefully a better version of who I was before.

From the moment I received my diagnosis, I dedicated myself to being strong for those who matter most to me. Pressing forward was the only option, persisting. And believe me, having two highly active young children leaves no time for self-pity. They, along with my husband, were a key part of me "making it through."

Looking back, I now see my tears that day in the doctor's office were a literal outpouring of love for my family and not any foreshadowing of my fears around their ability to cope with my diagnosis. My family proved more resilient than I could ever expect. Our lives are forever changed by my having cancer, but they made it through bravely, especially my children. Young ones have a natural resilience that too many adults underestimate.

My family is fine.

I am fine.

We are fine.

We did "make it through." •

Copyright 2022, Leigh Ann Whittle

Leigh Ann Whittle lives in Snow Camp, North Carolina. She has been writing for more than 20 years and taught college-level English and business communication courses for over 10 years. Her story "Listening to the Photograph" was published in the Personal Story Publishing Project anthology *Luck and Opportunity*. When not writing, Leigh Ann works as a marketing communication manager for a multi-campus flight school and homeschools her two young children. At publication time, she is entering her second year of cancer survivorship.

At the Ocean's Edge
by Paula Teem Levi

It was a sunny, cloudless October morning. A slight warm breeze blew off the ocean that made the day especially pleasant. My personal ritual had become to walk on Satellite Beach, Florida, on Saturday mornings, collect seashells, and then have breakfast at a beach-front restaurant. On this day as I walked near the surf, I noticed a peculiar something that was lying on the sand. It had just washed up with the incoming tide, I supposed. I reached down to pick up the strange object and examine it. It was a quarter-sized thick disc with a wide black band encircling its circular girth.

Standing near me, a pleasant-looking, middle-aged woman was combing through a strip of accumulated seaweed and debris left on the beach by the receding tide. This intersection of waves and beach is known as the "wrack." Such is the domain of "beachcombers." With a big smile and some excitement, she said, "You found a hamburger bean! You have received good luck!"

I was not sure what my reaction should be, but, for some reason, I did feel a sense of excitement. And it did look like a miniature hamburger. She went on to tell me that the "hamburger bean" is actually a "true sea-bean." And it was, in fact, my lucky day.

The beachcomber explained that a gathering of sea-bean enthusiasts was meeting for a Sea-Bean Symposium the following Saturday across the Indian River in Melbourne. People from the fields of oceanography, botany, and ecology—calling themselves "the Drifters," she said—were coming together to exchange their knowledge about oceans and beaches. She invited me to come learn more about the hamburger bean and its journey to Florida's shores. I was intrigued and planned to attend.

That's where I met Cathie Katz, a gifted artist, naturalist, and author. She was such an expert on water-borne seeds, many coming from Africa and South America, that others affectionately called her "The Sea-Bean Lady."

I was fascinated to hear her tell the story of the hamburger bean. Seeds, falling from tropical trees and vines, float down streams and rivers, primarily the Amazon. After being carried by ocean currents for thousands of miles and maybe for years, they come to rest on a beach at high tide during a busy hurricane season.

Cathie had been working diligently for years trying to bring awareness to the public of the plight of the world's oceans. That was her message. That was her life's purpose, she said. But too few years into her quest, Cathie discovered she had terminal cancer. Although fighting a valiant battle, she succumbed to cancer at the age of 53. We had stayed in touch and in an exchange before her passing, she shared a blessing, telling me, "Look for me at the ocean's edge, you will find me there."

This past October, I returned to Florida for a visit. Again, I was walking at the water's edge on Ormond Beach. Within two steps of the incoming salty foam, I felt a hard nudge to my right foot that got my attention. It was a hamburger bean! I reached down to grab it before another wave carried it back into the ocean. It was a beautiful specimen, still glossy with sea water. And, of course, I thought of Cathie. She often said, "Nature gives us gifts, if we only take the time to notice them." A lovely gift of nature had been deposited at my feet. And it was at the "ocean's edge," I noticed.

Soon enough, a young woman wearing a baseball cap approached me, walking from the other direction. She had seen me pick up the hamburger bean and she had one in her hand, too. She asked me if I knew what she had found. I told her first that she had received "good luck."

Thus, did I become the teacher. It was my turn to tell the story. The young woman listened with interest as I told her the story of the journey of the object that she held. She clutched her hamburger bean more tightly, apprised of her treasure, and thanked me with a huge smile for the science lesson. We parted company, continuing our walks in separate directions.

Cathie Katz's chosen work was all about making connections—between people, nature, the beach, and the exotic seabeans. They all connected for me that day. I had the opportunity to share the story of a journey and to bring joy to someone else, just as a sea-bean brings life across the sea arriving on a new beach.

As Cathie said, at the ocean's edge, a gift from nature. •

Copyright 2022, Paula Teem Levi

Paula Teem Levi is a retired Registered Nurse living in Clover, South Carolina. She is a member of several genealogical societies. Her stories have appeared in five previous anthologies of the Personal Story Publishing Project. "Who's That Lady?," appearing in *Curious Stuff*, was recently published in the Journal of the Burke County Genealogical Society. Her goal is to preserve as many family stories as possible for future generations so that they will not be at risk of being forgotten or lost forever.

Wild Mouse
by Howard Pearre

If you were a teenager in the early '60s, as I was, and went to "the beach," you may have taken a break from body surfing and ridden a rickety roller coaster named *Wild Mouse*.

Located at the Myrtle Beach Pavilion a few flip-flop steps from the Atlantic Ocean, it was not one of the big guys. But its vertical climbs, drops, flips, and twists were as heart-stopping as those of the monster coasters, just condensed into a much tighter ride. Its creaks and groans added extra excitement.

In Thailand a few years later, I was climbing into a Huey helicopter on my way to a Thai Army Special Forces camp when I noticed those reassuring words scrawled as a nickname on the back of the pilot's helmet: "Wild Mouse."

We sped across the jungle 40 feet above the treetops. After a half-hour jaunt, we came to an open expanse and continued at the same altitude and speed.

We crossed a river. Small herds of water buffalo galloped to evade the incoming threat. We flew over a group of men—

eight or ten of them, all with shaved heads and orange saffron garments—trudging in single file from somewhere to somewhere else.

Wild Mouse turned and grinned. I was young, as we all were. But if I was 21, he looked 15. I was glad when he turned back. *Keep your eyes on the road, Warrant Officer Wild Mouse.*

The training camp was near Lopburi, halfway between Korat, near the Army base where I was stationed, and the Burma border. Two of our guys were at the camp already, preparing for survival training, Thai style—ride a Huey 20 or so miles into "the woods," rappel from the helicopter to the jungle floor, and live for two weeks on turtles, snakes, bugs, and any other jungle delicacy you can "prepare" with a survival knife before calling for a ride back to the training camp. If you get bitten by something nasty, fix the problem with your pocket-size first aid kit. My job as an Army journalist was to write it up for the folks back home. I would sit in on some of the classes, interview the two US sergeants, and absorb some of the flavor of the camp and training.

As rice paddies glided below with rows of workers bent over transplanting rice seedlings in the muck, I observed a small mountain range in the distance. Without consciously thinking about it, I assumed our helicopter would continue along at the same altitude until we neared the mountain, maybe half a mile away. I thought we would increase altitude, comfortably clear the mountain, and then decrease altitude until we resumed the same tree-top-plus altitude. Wild Mouse had something else in mind.

As we neared the mountain, my mind and body were prepared for a gentle bowl-shaped ascent and descent, but my "ride" continued on with no altitude deviation—at roughly 90 miles per hour. I became anxious. It looked more and more like we were going to plow into the mountain. My body systems began responding, each in its own unique way. At about a football-field distance from the base of the mountain, Wild Mouse jerked back the joystick, and we made a sudden 45-degree upward climb. The helicopter continued to fly 40 feet from the tree tops up the side of the mountain.

At the top of the mountain, we did not level off for a gentle return to our previous altitude after passing the range. Instead, Wild Mouse jammed the joystick forward, and the helicopter made an abrupt downward movement.

My head was light. I gripped the grab bar at my side. We rode down the mountain, never changing speed, never changing the distance from the treetops. At the base of the mountain, Wild Mouse yanked the joystick backwards bringing the nose up again. The aircraft then continued at its same speed along the brown and green geography. Wild Mouse didn't have to look back for me to know he was grinning again.

An hour later we arrived at Lopburi. I gathered my gear and jumped from the door. I had not thrown up or embarrassed myself with other biological events.

For several days I watched snake-wrangling classes, sampled turtle stew, and got to participate in rappelling training. I visited Lopburi's ancient Monkey Temple where one of its hundreds of long-tailed macaques stole a pack of Marlboros from my shirt pocket.

When it was time to report back to Korat and my typewriter, I paid 50 *baht* to take a Thai bus. That included its own set of thrills, but would be far safer, I judged, than another "Wild Mouse" ride. •

Copyright 2022, Howard Pearre

Howard Pearre served in the US Army from 1966 to 1969. He is retired after a career as a counselor and manager with North Carolina Vocational Rehabilitation and the Department of Veterans' Affairs. He received an honorable mention for a short story "September, 1957" at the 2020 International Human Rights Arts Festival, and his stories have appeared in *Flying South*, *GreenPrints*, and *The Dead Mule School of Southern Literature*. He lives in Winston-Salem, North Carolina, and is a board member of Winston-Salem Writers.

Curiosity Led to Dad's Calling
by Monica Lee

Had Dad been a teenaged panelist quizzing his future self on the classic TV game show *What's My Line?*, he probably never would have guessed what his line of work would turn out to be.

As that long-running show entertained Americans by stumping its celebrity panelists with a parade of folks working odd jobs like banana grower, zipper repairman, and girdle fitter, my father was coming of age on a 240-acre farm near Bluffton, Minnesota, named for the bluffs of the nearby Leaf River. Dad performed all the standard duties of a farm kid in the '50s such as picking rocks, bailing hay, milking cows, and butchering chickens.

But Dad also got a kick out of figuring out how machines worked. Though he would probably be loath to admit it—he has always referred to himself as a Swede, like his father—I suppose this interest in engineering comes from his German mother. The first electric drip coffee maker? Invented by a German. That little sensor that detects rainwater on the windshield of your car and automatically turns the wipers on? It's from a German. Do I even need to mention

Albert Einstein? He was a German genius, of course. Dozens of concepts and devices have been developed by Germans who were interested in mechanical systems. Germans, they sit there and ponder the way the world works and then announce a fantastic vision with just a simple toggle switch or a light sensor or mathematical formula.

As a teenager, Dad contrived all kinds of personal inventions: he built a brake-light-disconnect switch in his car to evade speed-monitoring police, he disassembled and reassembled tube-type radios, and he even tried to transform bicycle parts and the gas motors from Maytag washing machines into a motorcycle (a feat he failed to accomplish, though not for lack of trying).

When the technical school in central Minnesota opened in 1962 with the fanfare splashed all over the local newspaper, it caught Grandma's eye. She wrote a letter to her son in Minot, North Dakota, where he was jack-hammering holes in the ground for Minuteman Missile silos near the Air Force base, and suggested he might be interested in the electronics program at the new school. This suggestion transformed Dad's life.

As a student, he developed a reputation for racing the freight trains on his way to school, justifying that brake-light-disconnect switch, I guess. Fortunately, his lead foot wasn't his only distinctive feature; he gained a reputation for having an inquisitive mind. Students were permitted to bring in personal projects to work on, and he brought in a turntable for playing vinyl records. He impressed his electronics instructor by supporting the turntable on two work stools and lying on the floor to observe the levers and springs on the bottom to see how it worked. "He always wanted to know why!" Dad's instructor said of him many years later in explaining why he recommended that Dad join him in teaching others and help pass on that desire.

That instrumental instructor at the tech school was Jim Lundquist, an affable man with a ready smile, a rapidly receding hairline and a firm grip who had started the electronics program at the tech school a year earlier. Jim grew up on a farm, too, before building the tech school program on his military electronics experience. Jim advised Dad to get some real-world experience before becoming a teacher.

Upon graduating from tech school, Dad collected that necessary experience with Control Data, a big company at the time based in the Twin Cities. After four years of flying around the country fixing the room-sized computers of that decade, he returned to Wadena and taught with Jim at the tech school. My father grounded students on the basics of electronics in their first year of study, and Jim instructed students in their second year. Their custom of team teaching enhanced their friendship and served them well as they forged a new relationship a few years later: they became business partners and ran the Wadena TV Center together.

An interest in knowing how things worked turned a couple of farm boys into teachers and then business owners. Dad's curiosity and sense of optimism led to a career selling and repairing a product that barely existed when he was born

Curiosity Led to Dad's Calling

in 1943—a box that transmitted moving pictures and sound of shows like *What's My Line?* into Americans' living rooms. And when I was a teenager guessing what might be in store for my future self, Dad's willingness to follow his curiosity inspired me, too: to work hard, to dream big and to follow my heart, a worthwhile inheritance for any daughter. •

Copyright 2022, Monica Lee

Monica Lee is a writer living in Jonestown, Texas. She has written five books including a memoir of her first marriage and an account of renovating a 126-year-old church into her dream home with her second husband. Her latest book, *Prime Time: The Sitcoms & Drama of a TV Repairman in the Land of 10,000 Lakes*, recounts her father's humorous and harrowing experiences as a television repairman in the last quarter of the 20th century.

Nothing an Hour of Surfing Can't Fix
by Randell Jones

Everybody has a story, and I was interested to learn his. John seemed a bit reserved, even tired perhaps, but we were connected only on a Zoom screen, so all our personalities were flattened a bit. Besides, he was a West Coaster, calling into the Eastern Time Zone. It was 8:30 A.M. for him, not exactly the easiest time to be joining in an online workshop to try your hand at writing your life story.

We were a small group of would-be memoirists, just six students and a facilitator. We were teaching each other mostly, applauding the good parts of each other's writing and pointing out the places that probably needed a little more work. We each came to the April and May weekly sessions with different expectations. John's were simple. He wanted to try his hand at writing. He was an executive chef, had his own restaurant, *Newmans at 988*, since 2006 and had worked before that as executive chef at *Stephanie Inn* also at Cannon Beach, a popular resort on the Oregon coast. He had the degrees and the professional accolades, the public following and the culinary colleagues to show for it. He worked hard but he had a friendly, easy-going vibe as well, sort of a "Big Lebowski" spirit—or maybe that was just me.

For the second class, John wrote a story, his first, he said, something he wanted to get down on paper. He thought it was a good story. It was, but it needed some work.

There's Nothing an Hour of Surfing Can't Fix.

It's Christmas Eve morning and we are in the beginning stages of opening the new restaurant. I tell a co-worker I'm going surfing, and she says, "Well, don't get eaten by a shark."

I look at her disdainfully and say, "Don't say that!"

I text my buddy Jack and ask him how the waves are looking. He lives close to the beach. He says it's about head-high, kind of junky but looks fun.

I say, "Cool, I need to call Brian about my board."

I call "Bry Dog," that's Brian, and say I am coming over to pick up my board. I tell him me and Jack are paddling out.

Bry says, "Dude, Lynette has baked scones and the in-laws are here. I think I just want to hang."

I say, "Come on, Dude. Let's just go check it." Jack, me, and Bry meet down at the beach, and it does look kind of fun. It had a little size, peeling left handers, and a bit of wind chop on it. But only two guys out. Usually there'd be 10-15. I say, "Come on, let's go get a few." We put on our wetsuits and head out. We are catching lots of waves and having a great time. As I'm duck diving through a wave, I see Bry Dog on my right paddling back out to the peak. A big set comes in and I take a couple of waves on the head and decide it's time to go in. We've been out for about an hour-and-a-half. I make it to the beach, and I was resting on a rock and taking in the beauty of all the surroundings when two guys are running past me saying, "Someone got bit. Great White shark attack."

I'm like, "WHAT? HOW? WHO? I was just out there." Immediately I think to go dial 911. And I'm thinking, *Who was it that got bit?* I mean there were only five of us out there surfing.

Oh, no, I hope it's not Bry Dog. Not after I talked him into going out. NO! Please, NO!

Someone had already called 911. I head back out to the break, and I see Jack and the other surfers have fashioned a stretcher out of driftwood to carry Bry Dog. He was bitten on the right leg. Had to punch the shark in the head to get it to let go of his leg. Then he had to swim into shore.

I say, "Dude, you okay?"

He says, "I think so." And I'm thinking about what just happened. The ambulance comes and we head out to the ER.

A few hours and 75 stitches later Bry Dog is finally back at his house. I say to him, "Dude, that was my bad. I shouldn't have insisted on us paddling out."

Nothing an Hour of Surfing Can't Fix

He smiles and says, "Well, there aren't many days you ever regret going surfing, but this may have been one of them. Say, are there any of those fresh, baked scones left?"

In May, I emailed John and asked if he wanted to work on this story for a collection of personal stories on a theme about unexpected things happening. He was interested and excited. He said that he and his wife were traveling. He would be back in touch.

By the end of June, I had not heard from him. I learned through a fellow classmate that John and his beloved dog, Remy, died in a single-vehicle accident on June 19, 2022, John's 58th birthday. I thought you'd like to read John's first story. He would want you to.

Be safe out there and watch out for each other.
Would that an hour of surfing *could* fix everything.

Thank you, John, for writing and sharing your story. •

Copyright 2022, Randell Jones and John Newman

Randell Jones is an award-winning writer about the pioneer and Revolutionary War eras and North Carolina history. During 25 years, he has written 100+ history-based guest columns for the Winston-Salem Journal. In 2017, he created the Personal Story Publishing Project and in 2019, the companion podcast, "6-minute Stories" to encourage other writers. He lives in Winston-Salem, North Carolina. Visit BecomingAmerica250.com and RandellJones.com.

CPSIA information can be obtained
at www.ICGtesting.com
Printed in the USA
JSHW040916270822
29809JS00002B/6

9 781734 796469